PRAISE FOR *THE HEART OF TRANSFORMATION*

This book reminds me how insightful Michael J. Leckie is as a thought leader, adviser, and change agent, both in writing and in person. Michael combines a deep understanding of the human condition, business, and technology. His focus on dealing with the personal aspects of transformation, and the six capabilities we need to succeed, makes this book much more real and usable than many dry, high-level transformation frameworks. Powerful stuff.

Dave Aron, Unthinker, Vice President and Distinguished Analyst, Gartner

It's not easy to write a book that is both simple and profound, and that tackles organizational transformation in such a personal way, but that's the magic of what Michael J. Leckie has done. No matter whether you're looking to change a corporation, a start-up, or a small team, you'll find both inspiration and practical advice in this book, the most important of which is to start with your own heart.

Ron Ashkenas, Partner Emeritus, Schaffer Consulting, and co-author of *Harvard Business Review Leader's Handbook*

Leading an organization through this digital revolution is a complex human journey. Michael J. Leckie distills his many years of exploration, discovery, and leadership authority into this simple map that walks you through the heart of transformation.

Mark Bowden, Co-Founder, TRUTHPLANE®, and global authority on non-verbal communication

Change is about choices, hard choices. There are six that matter most, and Michael J. Leckie shows you how to make the call in this invaluable book. Of the six principles he lays out, "Pathfinding Before Path Following" is the one that personally provoked me, challenged me, and opened up for me a new way of thinking about change. It points to the courage and the smarts you need to navigate a new landscape. In *The Heart of Transformation*, Michael J. Leckie provides us an invaluable map.

Michael Bungay Stanier, bestselling author of *The Coaching Habit*, and named #1 thought leader in coaching

Many times, discussions about organizational transformation focus on tools, processes, and structures, leaving out of the mix the most important element: people. In *The Heart of Transformation*, Michael J. Leckie reminds leaders that to truly transform, you must enable your people with the skills a data-driven world requires to both see and think differently.

Mike Capone, CEO, Qlik

Making a change in your own life is hard, and change is even harder inside organizations. Michael J. Leckie gives us a way to turn this massive challenge into simple and clear actions anyone can take. If you're struggling with change in your organization, then this is the book for you, and everyone you work with!

Dorie Clark, author of *Reinventing You* and executive education faculty at Duke University Fuqua School of Business

Transformation is an internal fundamental evolution of conscious choice, and when it's done right, transformation has an enduring impact. This book offers a timely and needed strategic playbook that forces us to examine behaviors and capabilities required to drive change and transformation, and how to recode our brains for change. It is replete with actionable examples and a must-read for anyone driving a change agenda.

Amber Grewal, Managing Director and Partner, Global Talent, Boston Consulting Group, and former Chief Talent Officer at Intel Corporation

Michael J. Leckie is a real person with real insight, and *The Heart of Transformation* is a refreshing read in a morass of business transformation tomes. Michael has not been afraid to make a leap during his career, always with heart and collegiality. This book will give you usable ideas at one of the most complicated times in recent human history.

Chris Howard, Vice President, Distinguished Analyst and Chief of Research, Gartner

Michael J. Leckie's passion jumps off the page in this guide to operationalizing curiosity and caring. We have to challenge ourselves to not get bogged down by the "digital" words of the day, but ask ourselves to get reacquainted with our assumptions and our heart.

Byron Johnson, Head of the Global Learning Center of Excellence, PepsiCo University

I met Michael J. Leckie when he was responsible for culture change during the digital transformation of GE. At the time, I was impressed by his natural humility, his "everything is possible" mindset, and his incredible skill to connect people together. If you haven't had the chance to know Michael personally, you will through this book. It is not a book full of words. It is a book full of life. It is not about theory, but about someone who has been there: humanizing before organizing, learning by asking powerful questions, and going where the fear is. I recommend this book!

Dr. Bruno Kahne, Vice President, Learning and Development, CMA CGM Group

Michael J. Leckie is by all definitions a true innovator. Humble, curious, creative, demanding, observant, and human. His years of experience in leading change in many different organizations such as Gartner and GE have been distilled into this incredible book of wisdom. He outlines the myths, the mindsets, the approaches, and the principles to help you lead change in your organization and make progress. When telling the stories of change, Michael is at his best and conveys very deep and powerful concepts in a very digestible and simple way. He will open your mind in so many ways: from execution to exploration, from knowledge to learning, from path following to pathfinding, from making change to creating transformation. I hope you enjoy the book as much as I did. Thank you, Michael!

Bob Moesta, Founder and CEO, The Re-Wired Group, and Adjunct Lecturer at The Kellogg School of Northwestern University

Michael J. Leckie distills his many years of transformation work experience into this amazing, must-read book. His insight into adaptive change and the growth mindset helps us see that transformation is all about people, starting with you, the leader. Michael brings a refreshing approach, showing us that no one framework will ever be superior to an amalgam that morphs to the given contextual challenges. It's not just about delivering suggested paths toward change, but actually starting with yourself first and modeling the change through execution. The lessons are also delivered with real-world narratives that make it fun to read and hard to put down.
Vincent Perfetti, Chief Digital Officer, Nu Skin Enterprises

When I first met Michael J. Leckie, I was deeply interested in how passionate he was about our collective abilities to help organizations to transform. We talked extensively about how learning could facilitate this as an outcome and the role of leaders in empowering this. What I love about this book is that it reminds me of those conversations as it is written in the same way. It is enjoyable and reminds you of the things that inspire you the most.
Jig Ramji, Group Head of Talent, London Stock Exchange Group

Michael J. Leckie has always had a way to take concepts that are complex and lay them out in a very clear and concise way. In my experience, curious people are unstoppable, and Michael frames curiosity at the heart of transformation. This book is packed with practical steps a leader can take to ensure transformational change can succeed. Curious about how to make organizational change real? You must read this book!
Jason Strle, Executive Vice President and Group CIO, Wells Fargo

Michael J. Leckie's quest for knowledge and his ability make very complex concepts relatable and applicable is found throughout this obvious labor of love. As the great conversationalist that he is, reading this book felt like having a conversation with Michael: interesting, thoughtful, and full of curiosity. This book teaches us great lessons about how to ask very simple questions in order to help us build open teams, tackle change, and to continuously learn.

Barry Warren, President and CEO, DHP Furniture, and Executive Vice President at Dorel Home

Michael J. Leckie's core premise in *The Heart of Transformation* is that when people in an organization can learn to care for each other, change can happen. It's a credo that he picked up in his time at Pepperdine's MSOD program and has been applying and refining in a broad career spanning multiple roles and organizations. But it's not a one-sided, Pollyanna view of the world. He rightly recognizes (through simple, actionable, useful, and relatable questions and stories) that as leaders and people learn to care, they must also create the purposes and management structures, systems, and processes that make caring and change sustainable... for good.

Chris Worley, Research Professor of Management at Pepperdine Graziadio School of Business and Affiliate Researcher at USC Center for Effective Organizations

The Heart of Transformation

*Build the Human Capabilities that Change
Organizations for Good*

Michael J. Leckie

KoganPage

First published in Great Britain and the United States in 2021 by Kogan Page Limited

2nd Floor, 45 Gee Street
London
EC1V 3RS
United Kingdom
ww.koganpage.com

122 W 27th St, 10th Floor
New York, NY 10001
USA

4737/23 Ansari Road
Daryaganj
New Delhi 110002
India

Kogan Page books are printed on paper from sustainable forests.

ISBNs
Hardback   978 1 3986 0010 2
Paperback   978 1 3986 0008 9
Ebook   978 1 3986 0009 6

British Library Cataloguing-in-Publication Data

A CIP record for this book is available from the British Library.

Library of Congress Cataloging-in-Publication Data

Names: Leckie, Michael J., author.
Title: The heart of transformation: build the human capabilities that
    change organizations for good / Michael J. Leckie.
Description: 1st Edition. | New York: Kogan Page Inc, 2021. | Includes
    bibliographical references and index.
Identifiers: LCCN 2021010233 (print) | LCCN 2021010234 (ebook) | ISBN
    9781398600102 (hardback) | ISBN 9781398600089 (paperback) | ISBN
    9781398600096 (ebook)
Subjects: LCSH: Organizational change. | Employees–Training of. |
    Personnel management. | Leadership. | BISAC: BUSINESS & ECONOMICS /
    Organizational Development | BUSINESS & ECONOMICS / Leadership
Classification: LCC HD58.8 .L42143 2021 (print) | LCC HD58.8 (ebook) |
    DDC 658.4/06–dc23
LC record available at https://lccn.loc.gov/2021010233
LC ebook record available at https://lccn.loc.gov/2021010234

Typeset by Hong Kong FIVE Workshop, Hong Kong
Print production managed by Jellyfish
Printed and bound by CPI Group (UK) Ltd, Croydon CR0 4YY

*Dedicated to those leaders who strive
to make the world of work a better place
for those who work for them.
To lead is a privilege, not a right.*

CONTENTS

ABOUT THE AUTHOR

Michael J. Leckie has spent his career helping people make sense out of the world around them. He knows that it is the stories we share that guide us in discovering what we might become and living up to all we can be. He has been sharing the stories of change and transformation for over 20 years in all parts of the world. In his work with Gartner's Executive Programs, he led the work to reshape what the idea of help truly meant to Gartner's CXO clients and to ensure that his teams worked with their clients to find the right problems, not just work on solutions to the problems presented. He discovered that it is rarely the technology that is the issue in a digital world, it is our ability to catch up to our technological advances, how we see that digital world and see ourselves in it.

In addition to his time at Gartner, Michael has held global roles for industry-leading companies in both people-centered roles and general management. Before forming Silverback Partners, Michael was at General Electric's world-renowned Crotonville Leadership Learning Center where he was the Chief Learning Officer for digital industrial transformation. In this role he worked to help a 125-year-old company transform its culture into one suited to a digital world—where change was a core capability of the people and leadership. He was also Chief Learning Officer and Global Head of Talent and Development for Bloomberg.

Michael currently lives in Connecticut with his family. He is privileged to have some wonderful clients with whom he partners to drive change and create the company cultures for a better tomorrow, and to try to fulfill his own personal mission to make the world a better place to live and work, one organization at a time. He places more importance on learning before knowing (you'll find out more about that in the book) and he strives to never take himself too seriously.

If you like what Michael does and says then feel free to reach out and connect via LinkedIn, his website, or a multitude of social media channels. If he can be of help to you, he will.

ACKNOWLEDGMENTS

Let me just start by apologizing to those whom I am going to inadvertently, but almost surely, leave out of these acknowledgments. I know that this will happen because of two reasons. The first is that I am absolutely fallible. The second is that I have been helped, supported, guided, encouraged, and loved by more people than anyone has a right to, and for that I am deeply grateful. I will do my best here but, if you are one of those whose name does not appear here when it should, know that I will realize this at some point and will try to thank you personally.

With that said, let me start by thanking Kathe Sweeney, Heather Wood, and the whole team at Kogan Page for believing in me and in this book. Your enthusiasm has been humbling and inspiring and your guidance has been on point at all times. Thank you to my guru of marketing, products, and all things media, Fei Wu. I appreciate your partnership and your friendship; this is how work is supposed to work. Thank you to Chris Worley for giving me the perfect love–hate relationship as my thesis advisor decades ago and thank you for the love and support relationship it has become. Thanks to Sue Mohrman for bringing me in to your world and for giving me not only your friendship but a practical Masters in organization design by proxy in our work together. To all of those who were a part of my Pepperdine MSOD experience so many years ago, thank you for the solid foundation of deep learning, strong practice, and developing my self-as-instrument (with special thanks to Miriam Lacey for telling me MSOD was where I belonged).

I owe a debt of gratitude to those of you who contributed to, through interviews, the writing of this book. Courtney Hohne, Barry Calpino, Rob Wengel, Joe Whittinghill, Bob Moesta, Erich Joachimsthaler, and others who have given me insight and ideas that show up in this book. And, of course, to my indispensable and dear friends, mentors, supporters, challengers, traveling companions, and men of great sartorial shoe sense (long live Jeffrey-West!), Mark Bowden and Michael Bungay Stanier.

From the world of work, my thanks to Brad Diede and Ray Piantanida for getting me started and investing in a supremely green young man. To Jean-Claude Casavant for being a great classmate, friend, colleague, mentor, and boss—your impact is beyond measure. To Don Martin for taking a chance on an unproven Montana boy via California with a lot of dreams and a little experience. Thank you to Ron Oberlander for setting an example and showing what a CEO could be. Thanks to Pat Pruden and Todd Antonelli for showing me how to turn what I knew into commercial success and for investing in me. Thank you to Robert Reiss for lending a helping transitional hand when I needed it most. Thank you to Stuart Levine and the rest of the team at Stuart Levine & Associates. Stuart, I appreciate your taking the chance and I appreciate the ongoing support over the years (and some really good wine). My thanks to my countless supporters and influences from my wonderful Gartner years; Alan Miller, Dale Kutnick, Jose Ruggero, Dave Aron, Chris Howard, David Meredith, and so many countless others who have, and continue to, support me. I can't list all the wonderful people who let me lead them at Gartner, but all of you made me a better leader every day. The privilege of leading your betters is something all leaders should experience for the humility and growth it brings. My thanks to Jack Ryan, Jennifer Waldo, Ann Johnston, Rik Dryfoos, Paul Fama, and the many wonderful and whip-smart colleagues I worked with at GE. Thanks to Suzy Walther and Jig Ramji; it was brief, but we met each other and that has real value to me. And thanks to great clients like Terry Waters and Gabriel Arreaga for letting me have the distinct pleasure of working with you. It is people like you who make my career choice such a joy.

Personally, there are some dear friends who are the kind of people anyone needs to carry them through. Mohammed "Khal" Khalid, thanks for being my brother from another mother. Geoff "Coach" Thomas and Jan "The Flying Dutchman" Schole for being my Team K tribe and kicking my backside into gear for a healthier and fitter life.

Thank you to my Mom and Dad. Momma Sharon, we still miss you every single day. You were always my number one fan and made me believe I could do and be anything. This book would have made you so happy. You left us far too soon. Pop, thank you for giving me some of your gifts, especially that of your sense of humor and your talent for telling a tale (completely accurate or slightly embellished). I'm sorry that I've become a better Casino player than you but that's just how it goes. One day you're on top and the next you're sliding down the slippery slope of slopdom.

And to my sons, Charlie and James. You make me proud every day with your kindness, your thoughtfulness and intelligence, your compassion, and the great sense of silliness and joy you bring into our lives. I'm proud of this book, but you're the best thing I've ever made by far (with your Mom's help, of course).

Finally, this book is dedicated to Molly. You are everything I could have wanted and more than I could have asked for. The elation of being married to you has lifted me up and carried me forward during the many times I felt weakened or defeated. Your laughter is my favorite sound, and I am beyond delighted that you are not only my partner in life but my best friend too. Words cannot express.

Introduction

Learning to Swim

It wasn't until I was well into my thirties that I actually learned how to swim. Not that I didn't go to lessons as a child, I did. I can still remember my mother taking me to Mrs. Rainwater's house in Billings, Montana, for swimming lessons. I mean, how could I forget a swimming teacher named Rainwater! I remember being frightened when I sank and choked on the pool water. I remember the fearful powerlessness of not being able to stay above the waterline. I remember the kindness and empathy I was shown as well as the firm push back into the water. And, eventually, I could keep myself afloat and move about the pool. It wasn't graceful, but it got the job done. And so, I thought I knew how to swim, and then never really thought about it again.

Fast forward about thirty years. Realizing that I am now a father of two beautiful boys who will look to me for guidance in life has caused me to re-evaluate some aspects of who I am. One of those aspects is my weight and overall health. I have become big. I never used the word obese to describe myself but, at sixty to seventy pounds overweight, it's medically and factually accurate. Realizing that I was not only harming myself but setting the wrong example for my sons, I decided to embark upon a journey to lose that weight. And I succeeded.

I did this by a combination of change in diet, reduction in food portions, and then adding in exercise. First, I walked on a treadmill and then I ran on it. At one point, my best mate suggested that we do some road races. He is a very fit Dutchman who has always got up with me in the Connecticut cold mornings to run, even if the run was one that he didn't need or that started his day much earlier than necessary. He ran just to keep me company and support me. (Thanks, Jan, your friendship has added years to my life!) But, in reference to his suggesting running a road race, my response to him was one of doubt. I mean, I wasn't a runner, I never had been. To which he replied that running on a treadmill was actually running, and that doing it on the street was no different. This was an obvious reality that I had somehow missed. Well, running turned into both biking and running until one day he said to me, "Hey, I know! Let's do a triathlon!"

Back then I didn't even know what a triathlon was. But he explained to me that it was a "simple" event of swimming, then biking, and then running, in that order. Well, I knew that I could both run and bike now and, of course, Mrs Rainwater had taught me how to swim. So, I thought, "Why not?"

We joined a local group in Connecticut that helped us learn the basics: transitions, etiquette, equipment, strategy, etc. They also brought others like us, newbies to the world of triathlons, to train with together as a group. And the training was fun. We spent the first few weeks learning and practicing transitions between sports and running and biking. Then it was time to swim. We put on our shiny new triathlon wetsuits and our goggles and waded into the Long Island Sound on a chilly spring morning. Our simple assignment, swim from one buoy to another, just so our triathlon coach could watch us and gauge our style and skill at swimming.

Upon reaching the second buoy, somewhat breathlessly I will admit after my wildly undulating effort, Pascale (my triathlon coach) looked at me as she bobbed in the surf and sadly shook her head. She said something to the effect of, "Oh no... no... you cannot swim! At all!" This was followed by other kindly but direct admonitions containing the words "drown" and "pathetic." Or maybe it was "pathétique"—she was French after all. Pascale was clear, but considerate, and she said that there was a program that could help me, and I was not to worry. She said she'd make a triathlete out of me for sure! At this point, though, I was now not so certain.

Nonetheless, a few weeks later I found myself at a pool in a small town in upstate New York on a Saturday morning, quite early. I was about to learn swimming through Total Immersion. Now, this is not a book about swimming (although you may have begun to wonder) so I won't be talking extensively about Total Immersion. I'll just say this: it works. At the beginning of that Saturday morning, I was filmed underwater as I swam end to end in the pool. It took me twenty-three strokes to cross it and my body floundered about with my feet dragging and my head above water, pretty much just dogpaddling across. Inelegant and inefficient would truly be kind descriptors here.

At the end of Sunday afternoon, I was filmed again. Now I saw my body nearly flat, my motion much smoother and quieter. Fourteen strokes to cross the very same pool that it had taken me twenty-three strokes the morning before! All I will say about the technique here is that it is a continuous build of simple behaviors that, in combination, make you a good swimmer. I cannot recall exactly but I think there were around thirty of these new behaviors that I had to learn and practice, which I did with constant support and supervision over those two days in the pool.

I felt triumphant at the conclusion of the program on Sunday. But, as the time was coming to an end, we all started to realize that these many components would be difficult to remember when we were on our own. Our instructors, anticipating this, told us the following (and I paraphrase here to the best of my recollection): "When it comes time to swim, don't worry about doing every single thing you have learned, just swim. You know how to swim, and now you know that you do. So just swim. But pick one behavior you learned this weekend and practice that behavior while you swim. Maybe it's making as small a hole in the water as possible. Maybe it's being as long as possible in the water. Maybe it's using your core more than your limbs. Pick whichever one you want. Focus on just that one behavior while you swim. And then, just swim. Next time pick a different behavior component of Total Immersion and practice that. And just swim. Over time, it will all come together, and your swimming will incrementally improve until powerful, effective, and yet effortless swimming is just what you do without thinking. Oh, and have fun, enjoy yourself, and celebrate what you're doing for your health and fitness! It's a great gift you've given yourself so keep on giving it!"

I may have romanticized my memory a little, but that is the lesson as it lives in me today—just start, you're good enough, and you'll get better as you go.

And, with that in mind, I returned to the water. And, yes, I became a triathlete. On more than one occasion I have swum the 1.2 miles that are required for a Half Ironman. While I'm not the world's greatest swimmer, my swimming when compared to the general population is fairly good. What's more, I am not afraid of open-water swimming and I take joy from it. It makes my life better. I did an open-water swim with Jan for 1,000 meters the morning I wrote this, just for fun and fitness.

So, why did I start a book about the heart of transformation with a story about learning to swim? It is because my hope is that this book can become your weekend in the pool—your "total immersion" in what it takes to be a part of an organization that knows how to change for good. I want to be your instructor, coach, and friend as you learn how to navigate and move decisively forward in a world where you may feel like your head is a bit under the water, or close to it, when it comes to adapting to the constant flux that we experience in work, which is only exacerbated by the digital nature of our world today.

As we go through the book, we are going to focus on behaviors— simple behaviors that you can try out and learn by doing. Behaviors that, if tried and then reflected upon, might just challenge your assumptions. Assumptions that, when challenged, may begin to show their cracks and shaky foundations. Change enough assumptions and you start to see the world differently and come to believe some new things. In an organization, when enough of us have new beliefs, a new culture emerges, and everything changes. For good.

When you get to the end of this book, there will be a lot of these behaviors that you have been learning and practicing at a rapid pace. You'll be thoroughly soaked in them. But you will "get out of the pool and dry off"—putting the book down and going back to your day-to-day life and work. When you do that, all I want is for you to remember the advice I was given, just swim. Live your life, go about your work, talk to your friends and colleagues, interact with your team, lead your organization, acquire and develop talent, do whatever it is you do. But, while doing it, pick just one behavior from the six capabilities in this book and practice that. Pick the one you like best or one that comes most easily. Pick the one that scares you the most or that you least understand or buy into. Create an alphabetical list and go through them in order. Put them up on a dartboard and throw darts to pick. How you choose is up to you. It doesn't matter.

What does matter is that you find yourself, in the very near future, confident in the fact that you can do this. You can go the distance. You can run the race and stay competitive. You can find your heart of transformation and routinely do things that seemed out of reach and you can do them with ease. In a world that is changing at a bewildering pace, you will realize that you won't drown, you are far from pathetic, and you can just swim. And you will find yourself comfortable, confident, and with a strong and healthy heart of transformation inside of you.

01

Getting Started with a Heart of Transformation

What is at the heart of transformation?

Let me start out by making a couple of statements that may seem odd for a book purportedly about organizations and how to transform them. First, this book is not the solution to all of your organization's problems with leadership, change, and culture. Let me repeat that but now put some specific emphasis on that last sentence. This book is not *the* solution to all of your organization's problems with leadership, change, and culture. However, it is one useful way to frame and address the issues that organizations face in building the culture that they need in order to thrive and also in developing the leaders they need to build that culture.

George Box said, "All models are wrong, but some are useful." Or at least that is how I've always heard this aphorism stated. Just a bit of research shows us that the concept pre-dated Box and that he used different combinations of words. Slightly apocryphal as it may be, "All models are wrong, but some are useful," is, well, useful. I first heard those words from the mouth of my friend, and global co-conspirator, Michael Bungay Stanier. It was a great moment of learning for me as I began to realize that things being "perfect" and "right" were far less valuable than just being useful. This is a lesson I have had to relearn many times over the course of my life and career (just ask my wife!).

By the way, if you are not familiar with Michael's work, I suggest you become so. It is eminently accessible and profoundly useful as well. Michael was a pioneer in making some of the great theories of people and relationships immediately actionable, primarily through the use of great questions. He did this with the company he founded, Box of Crayons, now one of the leading lights in moving organizations from advice-driven to curiosity-led. My work over the years with him has had a definite influence on me and my thinking and, as you will see, how the capabilities in this book manifest. Thank you, my friend!

Now, back to the other Box—George. What is most useful about his phrase is that it helps to remind us that there is no model that is *the* answer, only models that may be useful to us in finding *an* answer, or answers, that we can use. Even the best models and theories are only one way to frame a problem or find an answer. The way to judge models and theories is not for completeness, or their scientific accuracy, elegance, or memorability. While those are all great things, they are not the most important considerations. What is most important is whether a model affirmatively answers the questions, "Will this help me understand my world and change it for the better? Is it useful for me to do what I need to do, here and now?"

This book will present you with models and theories that are imperfect, mine certainly not the least. They could be more elegantly worded. They could be more complete. They could be more memorable. I could have cited more research. Of course, I hope you will find the wording elegant and memorable enough for your enjoyment and to leave a lasting impression. I hope you will feel confident in the research and scientific facts behind them. I truly hope they will be complete enough to help you begin to effectively address the problems or concerns that caused you to pick up this book in the first place. And don't worry, I will point out many of the places where there are other models that are more useful or that address things that mine don't. But, mostly, I just hope this book, and the models within, will be useful to you.

The second potentially odd statement to make is this—organizations don't exist. We insist on talking about them like they are something unto themselves, like a car or a machine. But they don't exist. A building isn't an organization, it can only house one. A corporation is a legal entity, it exists on paper. A logo is an advertising and branding tool, a concept, not a reality. Only people exist. And an organization is simply an organized body of people with a particular purpose.

I'll freely admit that the word organization is a useful word to have and use. Using it is certainly much handier than saying, "You know, that big group made up of Tom, Sacha, Suresh, Ana Cristina…" and going on to name everyone in the company. But I worry that, in our haste to make haste, we sometimes forget that organizations don't exist, only the people in them do. If the people (or their purpose) go away, the organization does too.

The people who make up our organizations are people who are complex, unique, hopeful, fearful, learning, living, and loving every day. It is for the benefit of those people that this book is written. If you are an executive leader, or manager reading this book, I am very happy that you are. It is written for you to read and benefit from, but it is written even more for the benefit of the people you lead and manage, in order to make their lives better, through how you lead and manage. If you are a student or professional who is studying or engaged in organization change, organization development, culture, learning, etc., I truly hope it helps you serve the people of the organizations you work with to bring joy and growth to their lives. Because at the heart of transformation we find people. Not structures, not models, not technologies, but people. In fact, for those of you reading the opening pages of this book online or in a bookstore and considering purchasing it, let me just cut to the chase and give you the heart of *The Heart of Transformation*—it is people learning how to care for each other, you might even say love each other, enough that they allow transformation to happen—to them and to their organizations. If you already believe you know exactly how to do that, that you know what behaviors are produced from caring about each other enough to be changed and help others change, then you can save your money. But, if you don't, then I hope you will read on. In *The Heart of Transformation* that is exactly what we will be doing, learning those behaviors that lead to the capabilities of change and transformation. We will be operationalizing curiosity and caring for each other so that we can truly and radically change organizations for good.

Why did I write this book?

You may be wondering why I wrote this book, with an emphasis on the "I." What was it inside me that drove me to spend the considerable time it took, to forgo other meaningful things I could be doing, to put myself out there for judgment (or acknowledgment)? Well, it's because I love you guys! I know I don't know you, but I love you. In his excellent TEDx Toronto talk, a good friend and mentor, Mark Bowden, shares how we are programmed through evolutionary biology to be indifferent to the vast majority of our fellow human beings. He also talks about the fact that we have a choice to be other than what comes naturally.[1] So, this is my attempt to overcome my indifference and connect a little bit more. Even though I don't know you, I want you to be happy, fulfilled, cared for, and caring for others. I think it will make the world a better place. I'll tell you why this matters to me.

About fifteen years ago, I was having dinner with a senior research scientist at a highly regarded advisory, testing, and consulting firm and he asked me a question. He said, "At our company, and this is kind of a secret, we have one question that we always ask people who want to join us. Not only do we always ask it, we are also hesitant to hire people who cannot answer it relatively quickly and confidently. Because, if they can't, then they might not be clear on their purpose and what their motive is for joining us. We find that people driven by clear purpose have the greatest impact on their clients and our success. The question we ask is, 'What is your mission?' So, tell me Michael, what's your mission?"

I was not interviewing for a job; I was just having dinner after engaging this gentleman in work with one of my business units. I was not expecting or prepared for this question. So, I was honestly a bit startled to hear myself almost immediately reply, "To make the world a better place to live, and work, one organization at a time." It was something I'd never articulated out loud, maybe because I'd never been asked. But it has guided me ever since, even before I ever said it out loud.

I started to write that this book is a culmination of a life of trying to do just that, to make the world a better place to work and live, but that sounded a bit aggrandizing as I read it back. Upon reflection, I think it is actually because I don't know how to fulfill my own personal mission, beyond the confines of the circles in which I move, in any other way. I want to be able to reach the people in my life who are at more than just arm's length.

I know that I have failed many times, in many ways, along my journey to make the world a better place to live and work. And what I have for you here is not perfect—as I said it is not *the* answer. But I sincerely hope it will help make your world, and especially the world of those you lead or work with, a little bit better place to work and live. I hope you will come away from reading this book giving it that high praise that I value so much. "That was useful."

Why another book on change or transformation?

Before we talk about change and transformation, I want to be clear that I am using the words change and transformation interchangeably. If you search the definition of change you get "make or become different." If you search the definition of transformation you get "a thorough or dramatic change in form or appearance." So, really, we use the words to denote degree or size of change, but it is all just change. I guess more dramatic change gets a more dramatic word. If you don't quite see it that way, that's okay. But it will make reading this book easier if you allow me to be slightly less precise with these terms going forward.

Now that we have that out of the way, we need to set the context for why to write another book on the subject of change and why to write it now. Here's my bottom line—there are a lot of astute observations and brilliant theories about change out there but there is not a lot of actionable advice. I am constantly asked, "But, how do I do that? How do I operationalize these great ideas and concepts?" This book is my answer to that question. I was asked it enough that I decided it needed to be addressed more broadly and publicly than in just the conversations I was privileged to have with individuals or groups.

I am asked that question because I have been working and advising executives and organizations about digital transformation for years. Digital transformation is still transformation, digital is just the context. But it's a big, impactful context. "Digital has changed everything!" is a breathless phrase we hear in business all the time. And it's true—it's just not the whole truth. One of the major shifts I see is in how digital has affected both the complexity and scope of change as well as the pace of change. That is why the need for a better mousetrap for transformation is so critical nowadays. So, before we charge into change, let's start by looking at digital a little more closely.

Digital transformation requires human transformation

The word "digital" is a problematic word. Like many things that are problematic, it is also nearly ubiquitous in the appearances it makes in our lives today. It seems that every company has a new digital solution or product that you simply must have (in their oh-so-humble opinion). The world of work is nearly falling over itself in conversations about the latest and greatest digital strategies for success—digital business, digital marketing, digital leadership, digital transformation, digital everything! And, with good reason, as digital is everywhere and permeating more of our lives every day.

When you do a web search for the definition of digital you will get responses in the billions—almost a trillion at the moment I wrote this sentence. If you visit the sites of the major consulting firms, as well as the boutique ones, you will soon come to understand that digital is the answer to life, the universe, and everything!

Ask any expert in digital and they will tell you definitively what it is all about. They may even have snazzy presentations to back it up. Ask the next expert and they will tell you that it is definitively about something else, with equally dazzling slides.

For some, digital is very clearly about marketing and channels, a means to connect with customers. Digital is now how you interact with the world. It is mobile, it is engaging, it is powered by artificial intelligence (AI) and machine learning. It happens in real time and it will make or break your ability to find and connect with your customers.

For others, digital is clearly about information technology (IT) and the systems that drive modern organizations. Having the best, most integrated, most transparent, fastest, and most accessible systems will give you the critical competitive advantage you need to beat your competitors and emerge victorious on the field of modern economic battle. It also comes in the form of "woke" digital approaches that disrupt the slow old companies out there and hold the promise of becoming the next amazing disruptor or technology titan.

Still others will even tell you that it has something to do with how you think, with company culture, with ways of being and working. You will hear about Agile, Lean, design thinking, user experience, and about how technology startups and giants are eating your lunch because they work digitally, and you don't!

The bottom line is that there appears to be no bottom line to what digital really means. My friend, and well-known researcher, Dave Aron, wrote a short, pithy post on LinkedIn[2] a few years back where he asked his readers to "stop hating on the word 'digital'" as it was the best word we had, for now. He said it was the word we started to use when the phrase "IT" just became too small.[3]

I think there is a lot in what he says. In my work with companies and leaders struggling to understand digital and digital transformation, I always ask them first to define what digital means, and will come to mean, to them. They need to determine which of the myriad meanings best defines their business and their strategy right now. Then they have to give real consideration to what digital will mean for their companies tomorrow and the day after tomorrow.[4]

Chris Howard, Chief of Research at Gartner, said to me, "Many leaders are simply exhausted by the phrase 'digital transformation.' And it's not because companies have conquered digital, far from it. Leaders are so beaten down and just plain tired of hearing of the glorious, futuristic magic of something that ends up feeling more and more ineffable while they try to grab it, that they can no longer stomach the conversation. More and more, they are talking about disruption and operational excellence instead. True digital transformation, because it involves changes to the business model, should be difficult and rare. Interestingly, COVID-19 accelerated business model change spearheaded by boards of directors and CEOs, so perhaps real digital transformation is an outcome of the otherwise miserable human catastrophe of the coronavirus pandemic."[5]

Disruption and operational excellence are also not new terms, not by any means. So why are they the new ones in use? Two reasons. First, they seem more real, more concrete. Companies know what disruption looks like and feels like, and it scares them that they don't know where it will come from, when it will come, and what they will do about it when it does come. But they don't want to be disruption's victim, so they are looking for a way through. The same with operational excellence. Who could argue with that phrase? It is the motherhood and apple pie of organizational life. The majority of the (previously) most successful companies of the 20th century built their reputations and their market dominance on their strategies and their operational execution. Simply, at its core, operational excellence is basically our fancy way of saying "doing it right"!

Much has been written about operational excellence and how to define it. I find that the definition from the firm Wilson Perumal & Company is one of the more cogent out there. They define it as follows:

> Operational Excellence is the execution of the business strategy more consistently and reliably than the competition. Operational Excellence is evidenced by results. Given two companies with the same strategy, the Operationally Excellent company will have lower operational risk, lower operating costs, and increased revenues relative to its competitors, which creates value for customers and shareholders.[6]

Like I said, doing it right. And I guess you could throw in doing it better than the competition if you wish. But what does that definition really tell you? It's good, it's clear, and I understand it. But I don't understand how to do it. It's like the old story about the judge trying to define obscenity by saying that he couldn't define it verbally but that he knew it when he saw it. If you recognize it, but you don't know how to create it, should it be your strategy? You can win or lose in the world based on so many factors that separating out which of them are directly from operational excellence in action is a muddled mess.

Clearly, there are some really great programs that emerged out of the total quality movement that purport to define operational excellence, such as Lean 6 Sigma, and these work systems can have a huge impact for good on organizations. However, my experience has been that there are more stories of organizations which tried to implement these systems with limited or no positive results than there are stories of great success. Companies like Motorola and GE which perfected these systems have not seen them guarantee their long-term dominance in their market. But for quite a while they were the *sine qua non* of success, which was achieved through operational excellence, in the eyes of many people, and they were broadly emulated.

The second reason that disruption and operational excellence are more in use now is that they feel a bit like cause and effect, symptom and cure. If disruption is as inevitable as it appears to be, operational excellence—doing it right and better than anyone else—appears to be the solution that we had mastered at some point. Focusing on operational excellence returns us to a time when the problems we were solving were clearer and more stable. To a time when operational excellence was everything we needed.

Please do not misunderstand me, I am not saying that operational ineptitude or inferiority are preferable! Yes, we need to do what we do right and then do it better. But how we achieve this has become much more complex. Today, technology has progressed to a point where operational excellence is no longer enough. The problems we are solving for in the market move faster than the solutions. Look at ride-share services such as Uber or Lyft. They started out providing the technology to connect drivers with passengers in the most frictionless way possible, but already they are focusing heavily on self-driving cars that will make those drivers completely redundant and they are looking at additional revenue streams of delivery that involve no riders whatsoever. Or Netflix, which moved from distribution of content to generation of content almost overnight. But as the world of commerce has changed around us, how we perceive and run our organizations has not changed much at all.

In all of these companies, the ones that are transforming and the ones that are struggling, there is one constant—people, not roles. Whatever the platform or the technology, the success of all of these businesses depends on some consistent, very human, capabilities. There is a certain irony in the fact that digital success is enabled by those capabilities or attributes that make us most human. If you ask leaders of the largest and most successful technology companies about what makes them successful, you hear a lot of talk about people and culture. Microsoft CEO Satya Nadella focused on people and culture in his reinvention of Microsoft. His excellent book, *Hit Refresh: The quest to rediscover Microsoft's soul and imagine a better future for everyone*, tells the story quite eloquently. Changing the employee mindset was his key to change and adaptation.

What are the skills and understanding that allow people to "fail fast," "pivot," "disrupt themselves before someone else does," etc.? If you dig down into it, which we will, you will find some things that don't sound very digital and are actually not about technology hardware or software at all.

The human capabilities that drive transformation

In the chapters that follow I introduce the six capabilities listed below, which are unlocking digital potential all over the world, for individuals and organizations. As we progress, we will delve deeper into what the six capabilities are all about—what they mean and how they manifest—and what you can do to develop and hone them as capabilities, regardless of your current role or work. We will also talk about the words following "Before" in my list. It is important that we understand that this is not an either/or, right/wrong situation. That is just too simple.

To frame this book, let me just give you the briefest overview of each capability and what it is about. We will define them further as we go forward, as well as explore each of them in depth. But, for now, this will get us started.

- **Exploring Before Executing** is about the fundamental human capability that drives change—curiosity. You will learn how you can embrace ambiguity without getting knocked off center. We are seeing this in the movement to be more coach-like in work interactions and managing ourselves in order to do so.

- **Learning Before Knowing** explores how learning is more important than knowing in a world where what we know is becoming irrelevant faster than we can master new knowledge. We will learn the questions that drive a learning mindset and culture. We will come to understand how people can find their blind spots, access their ignorance, and step away from their assumptions.

- **Changing Before Protecting** explores how our evolutionary biology drives behaviors of conservatism, risk-minimization, and survivalism, and how these predilections play out in our organizational lives. We will discuss how people can become aware of when they act without thinking and find ways to stand up, fail successfully, and prepare for surprise, not against it.

- **Pathfinding Before Path Following** makes clear that effectiveness used to be defined by knowing and following the steps to a destination set out by leadership. But we are in a world of a new excellence where we define the outcomes and then need to find our own paths to achieving our shared North Star. We are guided by values and purpose, and the best leader is the leader who is the right one for the moment, who leads through iterative processes to achieve excellence. Not necessarily the person who sits higher in the organization chart.

- **Innovating Before Replicating** uncovers how excellence used to be defined by our ability to scale and replicate processes, systems, products, and services. But the problems those things were solving are changing too fast for the speed of replication. The problems are now too complex for one solution. Now, excellence is defined by innovation everywhere, a growth mindset, and persons of tomorrow who think in all three horizons. They ask for forgiveness, not permission, and they take the initiative to innovate to build excellence in their organization.

- **Humanizing Before Organizing** is about the nature of our relationships at work and how we choose to see each other. It helps us see how relating to roles, and not people, is a major block to effectively organizing and reorganizing to get our changing work done. It helps us understand how to put people and interactions over processes and tools (one of the definitions of Agile straight from the Agile Manifesto).[7]

As we progress, you will read the stories of how some remarkable people lead with these capabilities, how the capabilities show up and make all the difference in their success and that of the organizations they come from. We will explore the simple, clear, and eminently "do-able" behaviors people can embrace and enact to weave these six human capabilities into their lives and work, easily. Finally, we will launch you and your organization on the path to the heart of transformation. But first, we must dive a little deeper into how we got where we are today—with fifth-generation information technology and second-generation human systems that are no longer enough.

One last note before we begin. You will find that this book is somewhat personal. Some of the stories are directly from my life and experience and I also use myself as an example (often of what not to do). There is a reason for this. In the end, transformation is personal—we all have to write our own story of change if we are to move forward. Transformation occurs individual by individual, through personal experience, learning, and change. While there are programmatic approaches to change (I myself work with major corporations on a digitally enabled program to build the capabilities in this book and change their cultures for good) and individuals are *always* influenced by their social environment, change is still accomplished through the heart of transformation that forms inside individuals—there is no other way.

Endnotes

1 Bowden, M (2013) The Importance of Being Inauthentic: Mark Bowden at TEDxToronto, YouTube [online] https://youtu.be/1zpf8H_Dd40 (archived at https://perma.cc/C5Q5-6ZH7)

2 Aron, D (2016) Stop Hating on the Word Digital, *LinkedIn* [online] https://www.linkedin.com/pulse/stop-hating-word-digital-dave-aron/ (archived at https://perma.cc/24XG-HHKD)

3 Aron, D (2016) Stop Hating on the Word Digital, *LinkedIn* [online] https://www.linkedin.com/pulse/stop-hating-word-digital-dave-aron/ (archived at https://perma.cc/24XG-HHKD)

4 Futurist and researcher Peter Hinssen coined the term "The Day After Tomorrow" in a very specific digital context. Read more [online] https://www.peterhinssen.com/books/the-day-after-tomorrow (archived at https://perma.cc/JY3D-ZGPA)

5 Howard, C (2020) Personal conversation with the author

6 Wilson Peruma & Company (nd) A Better Definition of Operational Excellence [online] https://www.wilsonperumal.com/blog/a-better-definition-of-operational-excellence (archived at https://perma.cc/M6AN-9SV3)

7 Agilemanifesto.org (2019) Manifesto for Agile Software Development [online] https://agilemanifesto.org/ (archived at https://perma.cc/3PTR-D3LF)

02

Why Does Our Digital World Demand a Human Solution?

Too many things to too many people

There is no doubt that technology is changing our world, and rapidly. It is impacting us in our daily lives as consumers. It is making us more productive at work. But, as William Gibson is often credited with saying, "the future is here—it's just not evenly distributed," and that is certainly the case with the adoption of work technologies and their impact on our organizational productivity. And, finally, technology is actually changing the nature of work itself.

First and foremost, the daily lives of most of us in the western world, and much of the emerging economies, are changing every day as we become acquainted with, and then adopt, new consumer technologies. In my lifetime I have seen the rise of the internet from something difficult to access that only an educated few knew about to the very informational, transactional, and communicational core of our lives today. What do we do today that is not done online or that has not been impacted by technologies that have arisen in the last decades, years, or even months? Not much that I can think of.

I wrote this book on software called Scrivener and then compiled it into a final manuscript on MS Word in Office 365, both of which stored it in the cloud automatically as I wrote it. I was able to arrange and rearrange the book with the click of a mouse, with the ability to gather all my notes, ideas, links, footnotes, and just about anything else I could imagine, all with incredible ease and simplicity. While writing this book was still difficult from a "creating something from nothing" perspective, I am so glad to have had the technology and not be writing it by hand or on a typewriter! No, the technology was great, it was the human using it that held things up, made it difficult, and nearly derailed it several times. The technology outpacing the people—we will most definitely come back to that theme later, and repeatedly. But back to the advances in technology for now!

Every day, I control smart home devices—lighting, music, video— all with my voice. Just a few years ago, when I headed home from the office my wife would be alerted by a "digital recipe" in IFTTT that let her know, via social media technology, that I'd left the geo-fenced area around my place of work and estimated when I'd be home— progress she could check by following my mobile device. Now, there are any number of applications for my smartphone that are so much easier to use and keep me in constant contact if I want. But at the time, that was a rocking tech solution that I was proud of!

My father is older and lives on his own, but I don't worry about him getting taken advantage of financially because I am alerted every time his credit card is used and am able to see daily what is happening to his retirement investments. And, of course, he can always call me from the bathtub just by asking Alexa to connect to me if he needs help or just to chat. Seeing the regular digital pattern of his life lets me know all is well.

If I talked to each of you, you would tell me about how you use technology to understand the world around you, take in information, collaborate and connect with others, share your thinking, create your brand, and make yourself more productive. You would tell me how you engage with technology as a 21st-century human being. And you could easily tell me how all this has changed immensely, almost day by day. In the time between my final manuscript submission and the first printing of this book, new technologies, or novel applications of existing ones, will be multitude.

Technology is also changing how we work. Most of the processes and workflows in our day-to-day lives have improved considerably through technology. Our communication is nearly instantaneous, our records are massive and immediately accessible as well as searchable through data warehouses, data lakes, or whatever data metaphor is in vogue today. We have more data than we could have imagined possible and that is allowing us not only to do better what we have already been doing, but to do new things as well.

Consider how incredibly rapidly the world moved its working life from the physical office building to the home office (or den, or spare room, or kitchen) virtually, via the internet, in the first half of 2020 as the COVID-19 pandemic arrived. Those changes, almost unthinkable before, happened in mere days and are still impacting our new world of work.

We have created entirely new industries by connecting things via technology that would have been difficult or impossible to connect without it. For example, connecting private homes and rooms to stay in with the people who want to stay in them. Bringing together private vehicles and drivers with the people who need rides—precisely, predictably, and almost without friction. The hotel and taxi industries that have been completely disrupted and redefined by emerging technology are just two examples among many, many other industries of the impact of digitally driven change.

We are seeing things like AI, RPA (robotic process automation), machine learning, bots, and other technologies change not only how we do our jobs, but the jobs themselves. Administrative and transactional tasks such as answering common questions or assembling components have been taken over and improved by machines. Virtual reality (VR) and augmented reality (AR) are becoming more and more commonplace in enhancing our jobs and making us more efficient and productive. Knowing things is no longer enough and we have machines to do the knowing for us. Now we are constantly learning and improving. No longer can we be trained, learn our trade, and just do it the same way until we retire. At some point, technology will enhance, transform, and even eliminate our jobs. And, as we have seen with the rise of the technology giants, it will create jobs—the jobs of building the new technologies, among others.[1]

So, what is the problem? It is something I mentioned earlier. As a friend, teacher, and mentor of mine has been known to say, we are living, and working, in a world of fifth-generation technologies and second-generation human systems. As people we have just not advanced in how we work at a pace that is even close to the advancement of the technologies around us—and this is causing tension and confusion.

The attempts by existing corporations to become more "digital" by providing free food, ping-pong tables, and unlimited vacation time is well-meaning but fails to get the results they are hoping for as the organization still creaks along bureaucratically (albeit with better snacks). The investments, huge investments, that they are advised to make in new technologies do not turn out to be their savior—the new lever that moves their world. Instead, they find that their company cultures are not "flexible," "agile," or "innovative," etc. They find that their people are suspicious of their motives, recalcitrant at attempts to change, or just playing dead and waiting for this new management fad to pass.

In other organizations, it is not leadership but the people who are driving the charge to work differently and leverage the technology now available to them. They want to use free-flowing data to take on more accountability, understand the work to be done to organize themselves, and digitally enable access to customers to define their products and strategies based on real-time feedback. But the power structures of the organizations are often seen as frustrating and blocking them. Too many meetings, too many layers of approval, too many naysayers. Some suffer in silence, resigned to the way it is. Others leave to join or start those companies that are disrupting the companies they used to struggle at. Still others just mentally rewrite their social contract with the company they work for and put in just enough effort to not get fired, but not enough to help the company leap forward. Many of them look at the ship and start to feel it sinking and so jump ship unexpectedly, leaving behind a growing talent vacuum.

We know all this. We talk about it endlessly at conferences and in meetings. We read about other companies experiencing digitally driven success and wonder "why not us?" It's the right question—why not us? Why can't we keep up with the technology? What is going on with us? Let's take some time to look at our history as people with technology.

The stagnation of human systems in a world of rapidly advancing technology

The day I started writing this section of this book, there was a small headline in my morning news feed about one of the people credited with having invented the internet and noting that it was now a venerable 30 years old. As I reflected on this fact, I was amazed at how something that is so truly ubiquitous in all aspects of our lives only came into commonly useful existence in my adult lifetime. My childhood was nearly completely without it.

But what was more remarkable was how it had changed in those 30 years. The pace of the evolution in internet technology, and all the adjacent technologies, has resulted in disruption and innovation on top of disruption and innovation, one after another. Whether it will be blockchain technologies, AI and machine learning, quantum computing, or something else (or all of those plus others yet to be defined), what is certain is that technology will continue to morph quickly and things that were not possible yesterday will be commonplace tomorrow.

Our ways of creating, organizing, and distributing information have gone through multiple upheavals in the internet era. The advent of cheap, effective AI will fundamentally change the work we do (and don't do) and shift how we work for good. These current and inevitable changes are inarguable and embraced by companies and consumers alike who are all looking for the next version or big upgrade to make their lives better and more successful.

We expect, and even demand, change, disruption, innovation, and relentless improvement from our companies in their technology-based services and products. So, why do we not see a concomitant change in ourselves and in how we organize? Because the fact of the matter is that our organizations themselves have actually changed very little since the time organizations first emerged.

A brief history of organizations

The advent of the modern organization, and any organization, has its origin in something that first happened centuries ago—when human beings conceptualized the concept of land ownership. Prior to owning the land, we just lived on it, and lived off of it, nomadically. Tribes hunted and survived on the land that they were able to find, fight for, and live on. However, there were no deeds to that land, and you could gain and lose access to it all depending on the whims and violence of nature and your neighbors.

When we started to own land, and when personal property became a concept we created, we began to organize ourselves differently. Division of labor became more formal. No longer did we all do what we chose to do—where some went out and hunted and some stayed home and prepared what was brought back—but now we began to be assigned our tasks by the landowner. In exchange for giving him a portion of what we grew, he let us use his land to grow it. (And it was almost ubiquitously a "him." Note that throughout this book you will mostly see the gender-neutral pronouns "they" and "them" instead of gender specific ones. But it seemed disingenuous here to rewrite the history of organizations as one of gender equality, because it wasn't.)

The familiar hierarchy of the family began to truly take shape and be replicated in the feudal systems that emerged from the advent of land ownership. The rich knight who was the landowner protected you and dispensed god's justice and you served this father-figure master. That was the deal, and thus was the organization born.

Today, we may have a little more democracy, in that we don't always have to be the son or daughter of the lord of the manor to become a leader. (Although in many places that can still be the case, with examples from the Middle East to the White House in the United States easy to observe.) Blood and lineage do not exclude all of those who don't have them from becoming the top dog. But blood and lineage still give you one heck of a leg up! In most of our organizations (and, yes, there are always exceptions, but I will be talking here about what is most common) the power and greatest wealth is concentrated in the few at the top and the rest of us accept what is our due, in return for our labor, under the good graces and continued employment of our benevolent leaders. Our ways of working are still primarily top down and mostly hierarchical.

Now, some of you will say, "Hold on a minute, are you forgetting about Agile and all the new ways of working that the high-tech and software world has brought us?" And it is true that there are companies which have adopted very different approaches to working and which have invested in much flatter, fluid, and flexible organizing structures. Agile approaches, and the like, have effectively helped teams create products faster and better. They have become very important ways of working. However, these agile teams generally sit within a more traditional organizational structure. And they are mostly in place in high-tech and software companies. They are far from ubiquitous in other industries.

And, yes, a select few organizations have gone so far as to eliminate managers (almost) and have teams be self-forming and self-guided (primarily). Experiments with these concepts and structures, or structure replacements, like holacracy (exemplified by the practice of having "no managers," based on the writing of Frederic Laloux and others) have certainly been explored, experimented with, and put in place. But they are also very much in the minority. Traditional, hierarchical organization structures are still the dominant model of the day across the globe.

But at least we don't work for someone who holds the power of life and death over us anymore. We can go where we want and do what we want for work. At least in theory. But for many people working in modern organizations, it might feel like a life-or-death experience at times. If you have been fired from a job (or downsized, let go, reorganized, or the like), you may have suffered deep doubt, humiliation, shame, and other negative emotions. Research shows us that some of these emotions, like humiliation and shame, register in the same part of the brain as physical pain. They can quite literally impact your brain like a slap in the face. Combine that with the potential domino effect of losing your source of income and, in the United States, your access to healthcare and it might actually be a life and death matter, come to think of it.

As a result of years of coercive and dominant practices on the part of leaders of companies, we created laws and norms to protect people. However, fear is still present in our organizations—fear of losing our status, fear of losing our power, fear of losing our rewards, fear of that debilitating humiliation and shame. Brené Brown's work, among others, shows us just how real and present this can be.[2]

On the bright side, a good number of our organizations are now becoming concerned with creating the psychological safety required to behave in the ways that are needed to embrace this nascent world of relationships over roles, self-forming work teams, and decisions made next to, or with, the customer. User experience and co-creation are now seen as must-haves in many organizations.

And what about the group that is tasked with people? What about Human Resources (HR), surely they can help us? Maybe, but I believe HR is currently at a crossroads of irrelevance and reinvention. As technology takes on the transactional and administrative tasks HR performed, we are finding that many traditional roles have shrunk or will cease to exist. Chatbots can handle those benefit questions. AI and persona-based apps can put choices about compensation and performance directly in the hands of managers. HR has a choice— become a project and vendor management group or evolve into being the group that truly understands and supports the growth of humans in the organization. HR leaders will not put training in place as much as create a culture of learning across the organization. They will see things through the eyes of employees and influence a growing human-centered workforce, or they will not be needed.

What all of this leads to is this—the technologies that allow us to escape the confines of our current industrial organizational structures and ways of working are advancing every day, yet we are not (for the most part) allowing them to do their jobs. Our human systems, our ways of working, just won't let them. But the interesting thing about human systems is that changing them is a matter of changing our minds. Human systems are a set of assumptions we have made, explicitly or implicitly, and we are behaving accordingly to fit those assumptions. If we just change our assumptions, or beliefs, then we can change our ways of working to fit the possibilities of technology in the 21st century.

It is that simple. And it is that wickedly difficult, because our beliefs are incredibly resistant to change.

But don't give up hope, there is a straightforward key to changing what you believe—**you have to behave as if you believe differently**. All throughout this book there are descriptions of simple behaviors that will help you and those around you to act, and eventually, think differently. If these new behaviors reach a critical mass across a given organization, they change the collective beliefs of that organization, beliefs that are the foundation of company culture. And changing the culture drives changes in the human systems or ways of working. So, what I am saying is that changing your world starts with changing yourself—the individual person. And changing yourself starts with what you say.

Talking 'bout a revolution

Gervase Bushe has said that, at their core, organizations are defined as who talks to whom about what. I must say that, after a career built on helping organizations in their attempts to change, I think he is absolutely right. While it is tempting to think that organizations are machines we can manage and manipulate based on diagnosis of what is working and not working, that model has not fared well in actually driving lasting change. Sadly, it has mostly resulted in cosmetic change that may even be a step backwards for the organization.

Organizations spend countless dollars and hours on change initiatives that generally fall woefully short of their lofty goals. Despite all the pinpointing of levers, design of roles, and campaigns of the new truth, it seems that how things work (or don't work) has a cockroach-like resilience that is astonishing. If you read the change management literature, both scientific and the not-so-scientific, you will find a broad and deep morass of "how change really works." However, not one of these models has proved itself so useful that it has become ubiquitous as *the* model for change in practice.

I am not saying that there is nothing out there that works, just that many of the approaches focus on structures and roles, and the redesign of the same, and that does not seem to be working. At least not enough to make a dramatic impact on results and business outcomes.

In the end, organizational structures are simply the rules or restrictions we put on who talks to whom about what. This is important because it means that the power to change lies not in structures but in dialogue—in talking. Talking is something nearly everyone can do.

The work of Edgar Schein (a hero of mine and one of the greatest thinkers in organization and management science) might help us understand why talking is so important to change. In his work on the roles people play when they are being consultative, he outlines three roles—the expert, the doctor/patient, and the process consultant. I won't presume to teach you Schein here, but I will do my best to summarize these three roles for you and tell you why they matter. The expert role is a transactional one where the consultant is hired for their expertise and they solve the problem and bring the conclusion or solution back to their client. The client can accept or reject this conclusion or solution or even contract for another. But, in the end, the ownership of creating the solution—the change, if you will—lies with the expert. The doctor/patient role is one in which the consultant brings their considerable knowledge of the subject to bear in the diagnostic process of asking deductive questions and then "prescribing" a way to change. This change is something the consultant can do to the client, with their permission, or the client can do for themselves, under the expert guidance of the consultant. It is more relational than the expert role, but it requires that the consultant have a prodigious amount of knowledge about the subject and that the client can describe their "symptoms" accurately (and that they are willing to share them all). Finally, there is what Schein calls the process consultant. In this relationship it is the interpersonal process between the consultant and patient that is important. In this relationship the consultant uses dialogue, mostly questions, to help the client figure out what the real problem is, then they figure out the best solution, and then own that solution. The consultant merely (but powerfully) creates the space for the client to change. But the ownership of the problem and the creation of the solution lie with, and remain with, the client.

There is much more to process consultation, and indeed all of Schein's work, to recommend. What I want to focus on here is the power of dialogue and the asking of questions. What is interesting to me is that the consultant actually has to know very little about the client or the potential solutions to their problem. They are engaged in aiding the client as he or she unravels all the turmoil in their minds and finds the true problem and then solves it. And the consultant does this almost entirely by asking questions. Schein's research has gone on to show that this type of consultative support is the one that truly drives the most change and leaves the client in a better place to deal with new problems that arise in the future.

All of this brings us back around to talking. It is in our dialogues that our organizations exist. It is in our questions that our organizations can change. This means that with the right questions we can help others change and, more importantly, help ourselves change as well. It is in the questions we ask each other that Archimedes can find his lever to move the world. If that is true, then what are the questions?

Good question!

We are going to get to that but, before we do, let's explore the supercomputer we are going to be working with while trying to change our mind, which is (of course) our minds.

Recoding our brains, for a change

All of the wonderful and intuitive applications and programs we use today (as well as some not so intuitive ones) are the result of people writing code. You may be one of those people. In one company I worked with, Bloomberg, there were over 4,000 software engineers at work each day coding and upgrading the software that runs Bloomberg Professional Services—also known to people in financial service industries around the globe as the indispensable "Terminal." The software engineers are literally coding and upgrading the Terminal, and its functions and capabilities, every day as the company works to provide more and better data-driven outcomes for their customers. But they are not the only ones who are coding.

Bloomberg, like many others, has invested meaningful time and resources in helping the non-techies in the company to learn to code in ways that help them in their daily tasks. For example, there are the non-engineers who have learned to use the programming language Python and resources like Jupyter Notebook and Pandas to create data analytics tools so that they can better understand the impact of everything they do. It also helps them to determine what really matters and what to focus on. It is literally and practically giving them a new language in which to engage the world and each other. And, like learning any new language, it was very foreign at first and took time to learn. However, they know that coding will become more and more a common language spoken by the rising generation and that the need to engage with the new worlds of data-driven decision making is something they simply have to do. And this is not just something that organizations who actually have coding divisions are doing. Companies like Decoded are bringing these skills to fully non-technical companies with great impact, creating the new breed of digital workers who work digitally instead of on digital products.

Coding, like any product or solution, starts with a need or struggle. It is usually prefaced with a sentence like, "Wouldn't it be cool if my computer could do X for me?" Of course, X is the task that helps meet the need or overcome the struggle. Someone had to give voice to some version of, "Wouldn't it be cool if my cell phone could just tell me how to get where I want to go instead of having to look at a physical map?" in order for Google maps or its equivalents to come into being. Someone (or a group of someones) had to turn that need or desire into reality, and they did it by coding. Using the language of code to tell the computer how to do it (and how to improve it through the coding that results in artificial intelligence or AI).

(While I use the term computer, which may conjure up an image of a desktop or laptop personal computing device, I am referring to any digital computational device or combination of devices. It could be your smartphone or tablet, it could be embedded in a machine or product, it could be sitting in the cloud working its magic for many more people than me. But, for purposes of simplicity, I will just use the term computer here.)

I said earlier that this was not a book about technology, but about people. However, we are struggling to find our place in our increasingly digital world and doing a little mental and behavioral coding might be just what is needed. We need to write in our brains the instructions on how to overcome our struggles, or deliver on our needs, in a simpler and less manual way. The good news is that you will find the lines of code you need in this book. And we will talk about the language needed to write that code in the magnificent supercomputer that is your brain. The other news is that it is up to you to do the coding and installing. Your brain is one machine that you cannot hand over to the IT team to upgrade. You have to do the work, which some may consider bad news. But I see it as good news as I am confident that, once you learn to recode your brain, you will make meaningful gains in your personal productivity in this digital world. Maybe even life-changing gains.

But we don't code the brain in Python, or C++, or R, or any other software language. We code our brains through learning. I am not a neuroscientist so my explanation of how the brain learns will be fairly rudimentary. The neurons in our brain are where our thinking occurs. It is the firing of neurons across synapses and through dendrites that creates neural pathways that result in what we call thinking. And, much of the time, our brains use the existing neural pathways we have. Think if you will (not to be clever) of when you are in learning mode. Learning is hard. That is because we are trying to form new neural pathways where these new thoughts can happen. And if it is hard to learn new things, then reflect on how hard it is to unlearn something first, to unlearn that thing we already know so we can replace that with the new thing we are learning. Creating a new path is so much easier than erasing the old roads and patterns in our head (and in life). It only happens when we have enough disconfirming information that our brains allow us to leave the old tried and true neural pathways behind, as no longer useful, and form new ones. Those "a-ha!" moments are the triggers that often allow us to build new neural pathways that compete with the ones we created before and that have caused us to believe something else all along.

When we have those "a-ha!" moments, the ones where we come to a realization or when the proverbial light dawns on us, those new neural pathways in our brains form as neurons start to fire. But learning can take a long time and a lot of repeated exposure to create, and make dominant, these new neural pathways. Recoding our brains for change is done one brain at a time.

The role of group dynamics in individual change

Throughout this book I will be talking about individual change as the basis for all change. It is my belief that organizational change is an outcome of a sufficient mass of individual change in any given organization. That said, I do feel it is important to acknowledge the role of group dynamics in individual change. The questions in this book that operationalize the behaviors at the heart of transformation are questions we either ask of ourselves or ask of others. While each answer is individual, these questions might very well be asked in a group setting, whether that is in a meeting or a workshop or even over a meal. Each of the individuals asking and answering the questions will then be doing it in front of others. That is a very different thing than answering it for yourself, on your own or with a coach, or asking it in a situation where you are one on one with the other person. Individuals are heavily influenced by their social environments. This is why so much of any truly effective organization development work is conducted within groups. As Gil Crosby has said in his excellent study of the work of Kurt Lewin, "Group dynamics are the practical doorway into applications of all (change) principles, and all of these (change) principles are present in group dynamics."[3]

While I will provide you with the questions that individuals will ask and answer, I do not go into their usage in a group, nor into the management of group dynamics themselves. While this is an essential skill for the change practitioner, much has been written about this and there are many people who are skilled at helping us learn from group dynamics. If you are a practitioner of change or organizational development (OD) in your organization, that might be you. If you are a leader, you may want to engage people to help you with a more thoughtful and planned approach to change supported by using the questions at the heart of transformation in your group or organization.

All that said, you can simply use the tools in this book as they are, in whatever setting you are in, and still be successful in making meaningful and high-impact progress toward your change goals. Just be aware of how the setting of a group can both decrease feelings of psychological safety but actually increase the pace and depth of change as well. The group is a two-edged sword best wielded with patience and practice.

How to hack change

Earlier I wrote about the idea of changing beliefs through changing behaviors as the key to culture change. We will go deeper into that later. We will talk about how devilishly hard it is for people to actually change what they believe. We will understand that it is not only extremely tricky but that it is a real process that happens over time. But we often find ourselves short on time in trying to change our organizations, so we are going to do what coders often do—hack.

The word "hack" has a bad reputation and often brings unsavory images to mind. But hacking did not start out that way and does not have to be negative or dastardly. One way that non-criminal hackers define the term is that hacking is simply solving the immediate problem with the least amount of effort. It is putting together something that may be clumsy or inelegant, but that is immediately useful and functional either to solve the problem or to learn more about it. That is my favorite way to look at hacking and is how I will use the term for this book. We are going to shortcut the rewiring of our brains with something that might just start out clumsy and inelegant, even awkward, but that will help us solve the problem with the least amount of effort. Something that above all is, you guessed it, useful.

For each of the six capabilities we will discuss in depth, we will also put a real focus on the hacks that will actually allow us to make the changes we are describing. Our primary means of operationalizing these capabilities, and therefore change, will be through our positive hacking of our own minds—and hacking is not nearly as hard as it sounds. Again, it is about asking the right questions. Remember that—questions as hacks. It will save you a lot of time and accelerate your own transformation, and that of your organization, in an amazing way. So, let's learn how to hack!

Endnotes

1 Want to know more? Check out Alexandra Levit (2018) *Humanity Works: Merging technologies and people for the workforce of the future*, Kogan Page, London. Alexandra is a friend of mine, a futurist and clear thinker who will help you see around digital corners

2 Brown, B (2017) *Daring Greatly: How the courage to be vulnerable transforms the way we live, love, parent, and lead*, Penguin Random House Audio Publishing Group, New York

3 Crosby, G (2020) *Planned Change: Why Kurt Lewin's social science is still best practice for business results, change management, and human progress*, Productivity Press, New York

03

The Challenge of Change

The myth of changing your mind

Changing human systems is a matter of changing our minds. But changing our minds is no simple matter. To successfully change your mind, you need to be sly, introducing your mind to some new assumptions so you can get acquainted with them, but not have to worry about believing them quite yet. The goal is to let new ideas percolate rather than challenging deeply held assumptions right away. You want your mind to start to feel a little less confident about what it knows. Self-doubt is a valuable thing for change, not the debilitating or power-sapping thing it sounds like.[1]

You might be reading this and thinking, "Wait a minute, it's not a big deal, I just change my mind when I want to. After all, my mind tells itself what to do, right? Aren't you overcomplicating this?" Well, when it comes to simple decisions, let's say choosing chicken instead of shrimp from a menu, I'd say you are right. But then again...

What if you believed you were allergic to shellfish? Let's imagine that you got really sick as a child when eating shrimp and this memory was so formative for you that you became convinced you were allergic to shrimp. What if a doctor friend of your parents even told them that this was likely the case, but that you should probably be tested? But your parents decided to be better safe than sorry and just told you that you were allergic, and that a doctor had said so.

While you have no allergy to shellfish, you believe otherwise. In fact, your mind knows otherwise. Your mind believes this to simply be true and this knowledge has guided your choices for your entire life since early childhood. So, "do you want the chicken or the shrimp?" becomes a much different question. A vital question.

Now as a middle-aged adult in this scenario, you begin to develop another reaction to something in the environment for the first time. You go to the doctor for diagnosis and treatment. During the course of the testing for allergies your doctor discovers a small number of things you are allergic to but, according to the tests, shellfish is not one of them. Do you begin to doubt your allergy to shellfish, or do you start to doubt the doctor? Maybe they missed something. Perhaps the lab made a mistake. How accurate are these tests anyway if they appear to have given you different answers (forgetting that you were never actually tested the first time)? But you know you will only truly change your mind after, and if, you start eating shellfish and nothing happens. Given what is at stake, are you inclined to believe the tests, or will you go on believing what you have always known to be true?

Here's the point: our tacit assumptions guide our behaviors. You can see this evidenced in our attitudes towards work.

Some of you grew up knowing that hard work and long hours are what drive success, and you live your life accordingly, dedicating more average hours to your job than the next person. You also grew up knowing that if you worked hard and did your job right the company would take care of you and that job hopping would only hurt your career. However, many younger people in the job market move around quite a bit. They want new experiences and to grow faster than their traditional organization is interested in supporting. They see stability as stifling. And all of this moving around has made their resume shine to some as it is seen as initiative and flexibility (not the instability others might see). They decide that staying too long in one place hurts their career prospects. Because your assumptions about work are different, you may counsel this young person, maybe even your son or daughter or a younger co-worker, against moving from job to job every few years. Yet neither of you is "right." Both of you are behaving based on your own assumptions about how to be successful in the world of work. And once you have these assumptions, it becomes very difficult to change your mind.

We abandon our beliefs very slowly, if at all.

The central problem of change management

Change is a small word for a big concept. As the old saying goes, if only I had a nickel for every time I've been asked about how to manage change I'd be a very rich man. It is a topic that has bedeviled people in organizations since organizations first came into existence, with great thinkers and many consulting firms writing and creating new frameworks and methods on this topic. In many larger companies you will find whole departments whose sole and express purpose is change management. And yet, no one truly seems to have cracked the code. Change is as hard to implement today as it has ever been.

In late 2018 I conducted some research and tried to summarize where we were in the world of work with change management. According to a widely referenced study by McKinsey, despite the fact that change management as a discipline has been around for more than 50 years, change initiatives have failed at a rate of 70 percent over the last 40 years that they looked at.[2] Nonetheless, most companies are still using some version of the same approaches they have been using for years.

Meanwhile, the pace of change of the problems we are addressing is increasing so rapidly that our long-term organizational viability will depend on change management approaches that must be exponentially faster than what we have, and these models are not even doing the job at the pace we need now.

Every senior leader should be stepping back and assessing the inadequacy of their approach to managing change. For example, my former company, GE, utilized their Change Acceleration Process (CAP) model for many years. The model was built at a time when the problems to be solved were much more stable and desired outcomes were much clearer and easier to define and articulate. The CAP approach is linear and straightforward—strategize then execute. This model worked well for the world into which it was born.

In our current digital age, the pace of problems is increasing so rapidly that we need change management approaches that are exponentially faster than the approaches used in previous eras. Unfortunately, a clear successor to the classic models has not been identified yet.

How the nature of change is changing

CAP-like processes or approaches are not fundamentally wrong—but they have become partial or insufficient. Why? Because they were created for a different type of change. They were designed for technical change. Technical change, or the challenges they address, is where the end-state or outcomes are known and can be clearly articulated and there is a clear solution—"if you do this you will get that." Technical challenges are those that require a technical solution—where the routines and processes are practiced and proven and can be taught to novices so that they can become accomplished. In other words, the skill sets needed to perform the tasks that solve the problems are well known. Unfortunately, technical changes are no longer what modern organizations struggling to compete in a digital world are facing. This programmatic approach is too slow, and the cultural factors are becoming more and more problematic.

Today we are facing times of adaptive change, where behaviors must change (often times to allow the technical changes to occur) and where there are underlying challenges to these changes that render our overt change goals moot. Adaptive change is an iterative process that does not stop and does not have complete clarity on the destination; there is inherent discovery or emergence in it. Renowned Harvard Business School Professor John Kotter originally taught us that change is linear—where the guideline might be summed up as, "don't skip a step, get to the end." Now, change is a flywheel that repeats. Change moves from the noun to the verb—as soon as you get near the end there is a new beginning. Interestingly, while Kotter himself and his consulting organization have evolved their thinking and still do good work in this field, it is some of his more linear original theories that have held sway in many places. Kind of ironic that his thinking about change has changed but that some of those people using his theories and models have hung tightly on to their more mechanistic interpretation of his original approaches. I hypothesize that is because those original models and theories are a better fit for the organization than machine theory, which is now proving to be very inadequate. It also may be that models of a concept, which are reductionist in nature, get picked up and interpreted out of context and misunderstood. If you want an example, do a little reading about Maslow's hierarchy of needs and how its common interpretations have actually diverged quite a bit from Maslow's intent.

Next, there is adaptive change. Adaptive change is harder because it is not programmatic, and because it nearly always involves cultural change as well. It is also hard because it is personal and must be done with an individual's engagement with change—their own change—to start with. And it must happen a lot more quickly than we have made behavioral changes in the past. Classic change models are based on economic and rationalist theories of human behavior, but recent research has shown that change is much more personal, emotional, irrational, and based in neurological functions and processes—many of which we are simply not cognizant of as we go through our days. Finally, most of these are linear models in a world where linear models move too slowly, and events are unfolding in a very non-linear way.

Adaptive challenges, and solutions, are ones where a shift in mindset is required in order to change. Ones where we must move to a more sophisticated state of mental development to see and address the problem. The simple way to describe this is moving from the "problem" to the "person having the problem." When we live in a world of complexity, we find that there are not well-established and well-known solutions. Even more challenging, the problems themselves are not clear and well known. We find that the complex demands and arrangements of the world require us to develop more complexity of mind to deal with them. Now, when we find ourselves trying to put the new wine of our complex digital world into the old wineskin of our ways of dealing with the world, we are not succeeding like we once used to do. In a world where the "What" is changing faster and faster, a new "You" is required to find and solve the adaptive problems of a digital age.

Leaders need to guide adaptive change

As transformation expert Ron Ashkenas notes, when it comes to traditional change management, "the content of change management is reasonably correct, but the managerial capacity to implement it has been woefully underdeveloped. In fact, instead of strengthening managers' ability to effectively lead change, we've instead allowed managers to outsource change management to HR specialists and consultants instead of taking accountability themselves—an approach that often doesn't work."[3]

The ability to guide perpetual and rapid change must not only be a priority but a prerequisite for leadership capabilities. Simply put, we have not given our people the capacity, competencies, and support to actually manage change successfully. We have given them tools and programs, but not the help they now need. And so, they fail to adapt and begin to lose faith in anything actually changing.

Jon Wheeler, a friend and an advisor at The Clarion Group who works across many types and sizes of organizations, says:

> Leaders of mature companies are often struggling with how to accelerate technology-enabled performance improvements to the core business while at the same time developing new technology-based business models. The historic approaches to change are not wrong when applied to continuous improvements or when the desired outcome to the change is clear. But in the rapidly moving and technology-driven world we are now in, these approaches are insufficient. Leaders must become equipped with the ability to also guide emergent-based change

similar to the way a tech start up approaches market discovery and value creation. For many leaders, "learn as you go" is a personal challenge and goes against the grain of what they have practiced for many years.[4]

Jen Kelchner, in an excellent article on change and digital transformation, says:

Real transformation isn't about tiny shifts. It requires bold pivots. We must recognize that sustainable change requires us to change how we think—on all fronts. Changing the way we think isn't saying that what we think now is inherently wrong. It means admitting that we can always learn more.

She goes on to say:

Change is never easy. However, with the right mindsets, guidance, and change tools you, your people, and your organization, will become stronger. *Leaders who model these behaviors consistently* [emphasis mine] and provide the right training and tools to everyone in the organization can create a culture of continuous improvement—one that, when built on openness, allows for the unlocking of the intelligence of people leading to the best solutions and highest competitive advantage.[5]

A new reality for organizations is that managing change and transformation is leadership's job working with everyone, not the job of HR or a consultant working with some specialist function or team. And I do not mean it is a job to delegate, it is an essential part of the leadership job itself and is, in my experience, the skill or focus most often lacking. Being an excellent strategist and/or operator is insufficient—but the majority of organizations do not recognize that adaptive change abilities are core leadership capabilities. Without adaptive change, organizational change will be mostly surface change. We have to help managers understand and make adaptive change because there is a big, bad step zero in change management in the vast majority of companies that is getting in the way—because all organizational change starts with your individual change.

Change is personal—and hard

Change introduces a new way of thinking, and most of us unconsciously try to make it fit within what we already know rather than revamp our underlying assumptions. Our beliefs, perspectives, and social norms greatly impact our willingness to change. Everyone is acknowledging that people and culture are the missing elements to change and/or transformation. However, what you can actually do about it is often stated at an incredibly high level or is hard to define and implement.

Change is personal. Period.

Yes, systems and structures often need to change to support the direction we have moved in, and there are clear operating model ramifications. However, we generally lead with these impersonal changes and, far too often, we end with them. Hence, change does not really happen. We pretend it does, but meaningful change in beliefs and behaviors do not follow. Core beliefs might go underground, and the tacit values of the organization will diverge even more from the stated values. But, far too often, as the answer to this need to change beliefs, what you get are organization designs and structures and systems along with the specious guidance, "and, of course, change the culture."

In a paper published by Deloitte, they said, "Remember, organizational change means changing human behavior, notwithstanding little evidence suggesting that behavior can be pliable or predictable."[6]

We need to be brutally honest about how much we have actually changed. To this end, organizations tend to make two crucial mistakes. One is to believe that once we have learned about an approach that now we are actually applying it in our lives and work. The other is to believe that the change we have made means we "have arrived," when in fact we have merely taken a first step and have a long way to go! To quote Bilbo Baggins, "The road goes ever on and on."

There exists a strange phenomenon that I have witnessed while working with both organizations and individuals on change. Often, if not usually, there is significant distance that exists between hearing about a different way of behaving, knowing what it looks like (or how it shows up for you or doing it once), and actually changing habits and ingrained ways of working. Unfortunately, we often mistakenly think understanding is the same as actually changing—we equate these in our minds and think that awareness has caused us to magically "leap the gap." Then we turn our focus to others and *their* need to change, as we perceive it, wondering why they are so resistant.

Finally, challenged with the need to change ourselves, there is often a lie that we tell ourselves, which is, "I'm just fine where I am and don't really need to change myself." And if you don't think you have told yourself that lie, you are lying to yourself.

Research suggests that people can be inspired to change, even in trying circumstances, when leadership can meet their psychological needs of autonomy, growth, and meaning.[7] One of the absolute best ways to do that is to demonstrate the changes we ourselves have made and role model not only the change itself but the process or struggle to make it. People pay a great deal of attention to what leaders do and little to what leaders say, especially if the two are incongruent. Change approaches cannot exist apart from the context and change they are intended to drive. The question, "What is the right or best or most promising change management approach or model?" is actually the wrong question. We need to first understand our role in change and that we are a part of the system, inextricable from the process of change. We need to have the tools and capabilities, as leaders, to drive change. We need support to build these toolsets and skills to use them. Finally, we need to recognize that leadership, and what leadership means, must evolve if we are to successfully drive change. Then we can affect change in micro ways all across the system, running in parallel, based on the same principles with people beginning to find meaning, growth, and autonomy possibilities in the coming changes.

Moving from problem solving to problem finding

Technology has increased the pace of change in our world. The problems we are solving for are far less stable than they ever were before.

Consider automobiles. For years the problem that automobile manufacturers were facing was the same for all of them—how do we produce the best quality and/or most desirable car at a good margin and win market share? The problem they were solving was clear, at least in their minds; consumers needed to want to buy their cars over their competitors. Manufacturers attacked this problem through solutions of automation (to reduce costs), advertising, and quality. And the race was on. It was a marathon and there were few major disruptions in the players or the game for decades. The quality movement led by Japan in the 1980s was the first real disruption and even that took a long time to impact US manufacturers. Had they been willing to admit they were not infallible then US manufacturers might have been able to respond more quickly. The problems were known, but the hubris of a track record of winning kept leaders from addressing them.

Today, everything is different—because the problem is not that consumers need cars. The problem has been fragmented and we have uncovered the deeper issues under "needing a car." Those issues are ones of mobility, logistics, delivery of goods, safety, etc. And so, we have Uber and Lyft and other ride-share services. We have the rapid emergence of self-driving cars. We have drones. We have personal aircraft. We have virtual reality and connectivity technology that allows you to be in more than one place at one time, at least as far as your ability to participate is concerned. We have scooters and bikes that can be picked up and put down just about anywhere in a major city with the touch of an app. All of these things are solutions to the problems underlying "I need a good car at a good price," because they recognize the actual problem is "I need a good car at a good price *to do…*" We have moved from a world of "what" to a world of "why," which gives us a much broader set of "how's" to accomplish what is needed.

This means that the locus of what truly matters has shifted from problem solving to problem finding. Or, maybe it is more accurate to say, that we have become much more cognizant that problem finding is more important because technological advances have made problem solving that much easier, cheaper, and faster. So, what do we do in a world where technology has rendered the old model of Design–Build–Scale–Execute as insufficient to the task at hand? The answer is: we have to evolve.

The six human capabilities required for adaptive change

In this book, I am presenting what I believe is a useful model to help you clearly understand the need for adaptive change and then engage in behaviors that have shown that they work very well in practice. This book is about changing your behaviors in ways that are remarkably easy given the enormous impact they will have on how they affect you and the world around you.

The model is probably best described as holonic in the sense that the new capabilities I am championing are built on, but not limited to, existing capabilities. The old capabilities are transcended and enfolded by the new. Not replacing but evolving. These original capabilities are still spoken about daily, in our work lives, as valuable and desirable. They have been valuable, and in many ways they still are. Those original foundational capabilities of executing, knowing, protecting, path following (in this case a strategic direction or proven path), replicating (or, in common organizational parlance, scaling), and organizing still have a viable place. But they are no longer enough on their own and can be damaging if their dominance remains unchecked. As a reminder, here are the six capabilities again:

1 Exploring Before Executing
2 Learning Before Knowing
3 Changing Before Protecting
4 Pathfinding Before Path Following
5 Innovating Before Replicating
6 Humanizing Before Organizing

We will delve deeply into each of these capabilities in its own chapter as we move forward, but let's kickstart this with the definitions we will use in this book.

THE SIX CAPABILITIES

- **Exploring**—to inquire into or discuss (a subject or issue) in detail or to examine or evaluate (an option or possibility). Here what matters is that we have a discipline of asking before doing. Not that we don't do, but that we pause to ask, "Are we (still) doing what is best or right?"

- **Learning**—the process of acquisition of knowledge or skills through experience, study, or by being taught. What is important for us to distinguish is that this is about the **capability** of knowledge acquisition—how we do this—and not the knowledge in and of itself.

- **Changing**—to make or become different. Whereas protecting aims to preserve, we are leading with the possibility of making or becoming different. Of course, this is not just different for difference sake, but for a purpose, which we will explore more fully going forward.

- **Pathfinding**—a pathfinder is described as someone who is making a way or finding a path, especially through somewhere unexplored or untraveled (often a "wilderness"). Interestingly, there is a technology-specific definition of pathfinding that has to do with the theory of the shortest path between two points and is related to maze theory. In short (no pun intended), pathfinding is about figuring out the best way, often a step at a time, and while you are on the journey.

- **Innovating**—a very simple definition of innovating is to introduce changes and new ideas. While there are whole disciplines and clear science behind innovation, I am focusing more on the mindset that you need for innovation, the idea that anyone can innovate, anywhere—you just have to be willing to question assumptions and approach the world with a growth mindset—acting on curiosity.

- **Humanizing**—here I am again going to rely on the work of Edgar and Peter Schein. The dictionary definition of humanizing would be to make (something) more humane or civilized or give (something) a human character. I am going to focus on the aspect of what the Scheins call "personization." This is not a typo: it is not "personalization" it is "personization." It's their word and they define personization as, "the process of mutually building a working relationship with a fellow employee, teammate, boss, subordinate, or colleague based on trying to see that person as a whole, not just in the role that he or she may occupy at the moment." This is a key principle of the Scheins' *Humble Leadership* and it is critical to understanding that this is not about being "nice," it is about building relationships to understand what each other is capable of and wants or needs—allowing you to collectively get the job done without the indifference, manipulation, or even lying and concealing that often occurs in work relationships.[8]

Living the six capabilities

What we find is that these six are very human capabilities, not technological or mechanistic. They manifest in behaviors that are clearly aligned with the beliefs that they represent.

As promised, over the course of the next six chapters we will explore how these capabilities enable adaptive change and just what you can do about it right now. How can you live like it is true and find out if it is for you? How can we make this model useful and use it as the cornerstone of transformation, yours and your company's? I will be giving you some simple behaviors to try out in the form of the questions that arise from each capability. Questions you will ask yourself and that you will ask others. That's it. All you have to do is ask these questions and see what happens. But there is a lot in the "see what happens" part. You need to have a way to reflect and debrief and then build those new ways of thinking and doing regularly so that you truly learn and live with a heart of transformation.

Endnotes

1 Interested in this idea of the power of doubt? Check out the work of Olivia d'Silva. Olivia D'Silva (nd) The Doubters [online] https://oliviadsilva.com/doubters/ (archived at https://perma.cc/YB28-AXEE)

2 McKinsey (nd) Changing Change Management [online] https://www.mckinsey.com/featured-insights/leadership/changing-change-management#:~:text=Change%20management%20as%20it%20is (archived at https://perma.cc/ZK8X-5QRU)

3 Ashkenas, R (2013) Change Management Needs to Change, *Harvard Business Review* [online] hbr.org/2013/04/change-management-needs-to-cha (archived at https://perma.cc/F67L-FFU9)

4 Taken from private correspondence between the author and the source

5 Kelchner, J (2017) Sparking Change With Less Pain: An open approach, *Open Source* [online] https://opensource.com/open-organization/17/8/digital-transformation-people-2 (archived at https://perma.cc/MSX2-2QAN)

6 Monahan, K and Murphy, T (2016) Humanizing Change: Developing more effective change management strategies, *Deloitte* [online] https://www2.deloitte.com/us/en/insights/deloitte-review/issue-19/developing-more-effective-change-management-strategies.html (archived at https://perma.cc/69RD-7CKH)

7 Ibid

8 Schein, E H (2016) *HumHumble consulting: How to provide real help faster*, Berrett-Koehler, Oakland CA

04

Exploring Before Executing

A story of execution

In 2014, Jeff Immelt, the CEO of General Electric, saw the future.

GE was one of the most valuable companies in the world and one of the most admired. It was that rare company that had withstood the test of time and maintained a position of leadership in the Dow Jones Index while so many had risen and fallen. GE's famed management development program was considered the finest in the world, known to be a leader in the development of leaders. Crotonville, located in Ossining, New York, was the core of the culture and a place where Immelt never failed to meet with those newly promoted, and occasionally newly hired, into the Executive Band—a top 5 percent position that could open doors to companies all over the world looking to benefit from the GE leadership talent machine. GE was a company to be admired.

I first encountered Jeff Immelt and GE when working with the global advisory firm Gartner. Dozens of GE executives were members in Gartner's Executive Programs service, which is the largest network of chief information officers, chief digital officers, and chief technology officers in the world. GE technology leaders were both big participants and big contributors to the network and I had the pleasure of knowing many of them. In 2015 and early 2016, I found myself regularly meeting with GE leadership across all areas and functions as they began their quest to transform into what Immelt called a "digital industrial" company. As the cultures of the Silicon Valley, GE's Fairfield County Connecticut Headquarters and GE Capital, and that of Schenectady, New York (the heart of manufacturing and development), began to come together, GE leadership was trying to determine the best way to lead in this new, digital world. Talking with leaders about this was what I found myself doing.

After doing this for some time, I was asked to join GE in early 2016 as Chief Learning Officer for the digital industrial transformation, with a remit to help build the organizational culture and leadership culture needed for a digital world. Much of what was tested and discovered there has found its way into this book or has helped in the development of these capabilities.

I left GE in 2018 when John Flannery was in charge for his short tenure and when the focus on digital, as it had been, had shifted. While I have met Jeff Immelt several times and spoken with him, I was not spending my time in his day-to-day circles either before or after I joined GE. But I was working closely with those who did, especially those who were driving both the digital agenda and the leadership agenda. And while I have seen GE's fortunes rise and fall it does not dim my admiration for what Immelt and GE leadership were trying to do in becoming a digital industrial and vying to become the leading platform for the industrial internet of things (IIoT). I still think that the strategy had real foresight. I will try to explain it in brief as it is a story that will help set the stage for looking at Exploring over Executing.

Becoming a digital industrial

In 2016, GE's businesses, roughly speaking, had two major commercial components—the production of big, technically elegant and innovative machines and the servicing of those machines. Yes, there were the lighting and appliances businesses, but these were being sold off in the anticipation of focusing on the big industrials: jet engines, nuclear power generation, wind turbines, locomotives, MRIs, etc., and the software that would transform them.

Whereas the value of the machines was originally what mattered most, the margins on the sale of industrial machines were getting squeezed and were going to continue to get squeezed. In a world of rapidly advancing technology, even the most intricate machines would ineluctably move toward commodity goods. Some of this was due to the rise in what is called additive manufacturing. You probably know of this as 3-D printing. What you may not know is that you can 3-D print large, complicated metal machinery, which can add strength while simultaneously eliminating weight. Moving from casting metal parts to printing them continues to have a major impact on manufacturing. Another factor was the emergence of big data and predictive analytics, which would cause a shift away from the value *of* a machine being important to the value *from* a machine being important. Let me explain what I mean by that.

A jet engine was a valuable product, a technological marvel, but the differences between jet engines made by GE or Rolls-Royce or others were, in the end, not drastically different. The core technology was established. You could fly your planes on any of them, you just needed the best deal in order to keep your costs down. The margins on the engines got smaller.

However, these engines did require service, both by regulatory demand and for the longevity of the big investment in each engine, not to mention passenger safety. Over time, the services side of the business grew to be much more profitable than just the selling of the engines. Think of your car, if you own one. You buy the car and, depending on the situation, the dealer makes some money or a little, or maybe none if the car is a loss leader to drive volume or serve some other purpose such as to remediate too much inventory. But the service, well, that is where the money is made. Bringing in the car over and over to maintain it provides tremendous value to dealerships.

So, GE had wisely also built up a world-class services business for the big, beautiful machines it sold. But then, big data came along as did the advances in sensors, combined with a dropping cost of making them and an increasing ability to crunch big data due to increased computing power. So what? Let's go back to our car. What if we didn't just take the car in when service was "due" either per the manual or the warning indicators built into the car? What if the following is what happened?

You wake up one morning and get into your car to commute to the office. As you are leaving your car speaks up. "Hey, good morning, I hope you have a great drive today. I just wanted to let you know that I have determined that I need some servicing due to the wear and tear my sensors are sensing. I checked your calendar, via my onboard link to the internet, and know that you are going to drive me to the airport next Tuesday and leave me there for a couple of days (no hard feelings, mind you). So, I checked with some service stations in the area of the airport, cross-referenced those with internet-based evaluations of service quality and pricing, and have selected one that had an appointment time during your travels. If you're okay with it, I'll drive myself there after I drop you off, then come back and park and activate a beacon on my app for when you arrive to tell you where I am. Sound okay?"

A few short years ago that would have been science fiction. Not anymore. And I tell you the car story because it illustrates what was coming for jet engines. Modern jet engines have over 140 sensors on them and growing. Digital technology can monitor everything happening to that engine in all conditions and ascertain, while it is flying, what is happening to it, how usage and the environment are impacting its performance, and what services it might need and when. Each engine could have a digital twin that showed us exactly what was happening to the engine at all times, even while flying over oceans and deserts. Predictive analytics would be able to anticipate the engine's needs and identify only the needs actually needed. There would be no more requirement for "regularly scheduled" maintenance. Maintenance could now be just right and just in time.

If a jet engine could tell you when it needed servicing, and could get bids, select providers, schedule and arrange for the servicing itself, then the revenue that GE currently got from the cost of servicing would drop dramatically in both scope of servicing and frequency. And this was not limited to jet engines, there was an analogous story for GE's other industrial equipment.

Immelt saw the risk to their current business model and realized that the future was digital. In looking at the consumer internet of things (IoT) and listening to those around him who were beginning to visualize the industrial internet of things (IIoT), he saw that GE had an opportunity. GE could provide the platform for the IIoT. And not just for GE, but for their competitors' equipment as well.

GE could become the world's first "digital-industrial" company. Immelt proclaimed in 2014 that GE would be a "top 10 software company" by 2020, with US $4 billion in annual revenue from its new Predix software alone.[1] The vision was for GE to become a software company. More precisely, to become the platform, or platform as a service (PaaS), for the IIoT—and their Predix software would be that platform.

According to various studies at the time, the size of the IIoT market was somewhere between US $600 billion and over $1 trillion. It would dwarf the consumer IoT. The opportunity, and the threat, were of a scale not seen before—and GE was positioned to lead.

GE was a company known for its ability to execute. The former CEO Larry Bossidy wrote what is arguably considered the definitive book on the topic, *Execution: The discipline of getting things done* (2002). He learned it all working at GE with another legend of corporate America, Jack Welch, the veritable poster child of execution. Their formula was simple: hire the best people, train them better than anyone else, let the best of them create brilliant strategies, and then let their teams of overachievers execute those strategies with gusto.

So, when Immelt lit upon the idea to leverage GE's scale and skills to build the platform for the IIoT better and faster than anyone else, it was seen as a brilliant move by many. GE could acquire skilled people to develop software for machines for which they had the most domain knowledge. During this time, I often said that you didn't need to be an ornithologist to build angry birds (which was a huge deal back then), but it was a lot harder to build software that could learn, understand, and conduct predictive analysis for jet engines or wind turbines if you didn't understand how they were built, how they ran, what they were made of, how they reacted, and where they were going. GE already had the domain knowledge, so their goal was to hire the software skills. With that in mind, Immelt hired Bill Ruh from Cisco in 2014 and, subsequently, they opened up shop east of the Silicon Valley in San Ramon, California. The new GE Digital team began hiring experienced software developers and began to develop in earnest.

GE had a plan. Many believed GE had the right plan—and GE had the most resources of its industrial competitors and was out of the gate first. The story of GE's rise and fall is well documented in *Lights Out: Pride, delusion, and the fall of General Electric* (2020) by Thomas Gryta and Ted Mann. And, while I find their story to have some sharp edges to it, they do chronicle well the tumultuous time at which I worked both with GE and then at GE. It was a time that saw something unprecedented in GE history because in 2018, after a mere year-long tenure by John Flannery, an outside CEO who was not raised in the GE way was put in charge. Larry Culp, former Danaher CEO, became the GE CEO. As for GE Digital, it is much smaller and Bill Ruh and most of the leadership from my time have gone on to key leadership roles in other successful companies. The execution of a brilliant plan to transform GE into a digital industrial and to become a top-10 software company has not come to pass. GE sold off businesses and became a company in turnaround.

I don't purport to be able to tell you the whole story of why this once household name needed to be turned around; Gryta and Mann have documented much of what went on. But there is something that I saw that I believe is also a part of the story. I sat in the middle of this situation for two years, and observed closely for several years before, and I believe the focus on execution, and a lack of exploration, was one of the contributing factors in what turned GE's digital dream into a business nightmare.

You see, once the strategy was set it was handed over to be executed. Remember, the magic formula was the best strategy plus the best execution equals the best outcome. GE's systems and processes were set up to get things done! I have a friend who cautions his clients against "the seductive lure of getting things done" and GE was a getting-things-done machine. "What did you deliver?" "What did you put on the table?" These were the questions a GE manager asked, especially come performance review time or, more precisely, rewards distribution time.

So, when GE found themselves needing to build a software company, they got it done and got it done fast. When they needed to build software, they delivered software. The problem with such a laser-like focus on execution is that it didn't account for disparities that arise when you are doing something you've never done in the same way you've always done things before. The people on the software side did not agree on how to build software, and the software was not as scalable as it needed to be as much of it was customized for customers. This meant that it was not something that could readily be resold to another buyer. For this and other reasons, the software product could not quite deliver on the promises they made in the market.[2]

The focus on speed to market may have prevented leaders from asking questions that could have helped improve processes. But did they step back to ask if building a company at pace was the best way to build a new company? Now, the question of if the organization needed to collaborate across organizational boundaries better was discussed, but we were slow in addressing it in a system where these entities operated so separately. Remember, GE itself was comprised of what would have been several Fortune 500 firms on their own! We talked about what people were being rewarded for doing and if it was aligned to what they were being told to do from the top, but we struggled to address wholesale change to entrenched reward and recognition systems quickly. In a system the size of GE, it is always easy to get bogged down in politics and competing priorities. So, mostly people focused on what they could—executing. GE invested billions in executing on a great strategy. And it might still have worked, if they'd had the time to step back, explore what was happening, and consider if there was another way. But then along came a perfect storm of financial missteps and plain bad luck that piled misery upon misery and GE's time at the top came to an abrupt halt. A corporate fire sale commenced, and nothing would ever be the same as the company lost well in excess of US $100 billion of market valuation in a single year.

Execution had potentially taken on a much darker meaning as divisions were sold and jobs were lost.

What is execution?

So, what is "execution"? For our purposes, I am using the connotation of the word as used in the business world—to execute means to carry out or put into effect a plan, order, or course of action. Now, what is wrong with that? Why wouldn't you value carrying out or putting into effect a plan, especially a good one? Isn't that what organizations are built to do—carry out plans effectively? And I am not saying that putting into effect a plan or course of action is not important, of course it is. Without planning it would be very hard to make progress in large groups or organizations. But how we plan, who does the planning, and how closely linked or overlapped the planning are and executing are the questions we need to address.

My biggest concern with the linear strategize/plan then execute model is that it simply no longer moves fast enough for the digital world we live in today. This approach was built for, and thrived in, the good old days of relative stability. Yet most of our organizations still seem to be operating as if they had all the time in the world and could stay in the same planning patterns and business cycles that they have had for years. Legacy organizations are getting disrupted left and right and entire industries are disappearing or being replaced by their digital successors. Do these disrupting organizations lead with execution? No, they do not. They value exploring before executing, which is how they are able to innovate and, in many cases, reinvent themselves while they are still successful.

Execution requires compliance. Once the systems and processes are defined and put in place, an execution focus requires close compliance with those systems and processes to work effectively and efficiently. But compliance is a double-edged sword. It may make the systems and processes flow efficiently and effectively but it reinforces the virtue of compliance for our employees. While the original intention is to comply with the systems and processes to achieve the outcomes that could be best achieved through those systems and processes, our compliant employees begin to just focus on the systems and processes themselves. What you get then, sooner or later, is excellent execution that can be disconnected from the outcome. Execution must be accompanied by the knowledge of what that execution is achieving as an outcome—for customers, for employees, for the company, and (just maybe) for the world we live in.

Execution focused businesses today are largely still leveraging the systems and processes that they have used before effectively and efficiently. Most of the time we refer to these as best practices or "proven" processes and we take comfort in our belief that if we just do what is "right" then everything will work out okay.

The problem with repeated execution of our "proven" systems and processes is that it leads to us stopping the practice of questioning whether our systems and processes are still what we need. When problems were more stable and less complex, this was a less urgent question. Today, we cannot overemphasize its urgency. Reliance on our systems and processes has resulted in a failure to learn. Instead, we spend all of our time following and doing; we spend it executing.

Learning comes from questioning and then finding out. If all we do is follow our systems and processes without questioning their viability, then we have execution without evolution. The systems and processes that were once useful become a crutch that keeps us from improving. The world of work is littered with the sad memory of organizations that tried to stick with what worked, no matter what, and died a slow death because of it.

So, what are we to do? We have to now start with exploration. What do I mean by exploration? You don't need a pith helmet or a machete to do it (most of the time). What you need is a willingness to go back and go forward.

Going back means asking the questions, "What are our systems and processes set up to accomplish in the first place? What was their intention? Why were they needed? What made them useful?" Once we go back and ask those questions we can then go forward and ask, "Are these systems and processes still the best way to solve the problems they are solving? How do we know? What are we not seeing?

Who can help us answer these questions? What might the new solutions be and are they just a tweak or a major rethinking?" All of these questions can help us explore the current value of our systems and processes and determine if there is now a better way.

Sometimes there is not. Sometimes the systems and processes we have remain the best solutions for solving our problems. But we must realize that the frequency of that being the case is diminishing.

The discipline of exploring helps us build this new organizational muscle. It helps us see ahead of others, or before it is too late, when our executing is no longer getting the job done and exploring can help us change how we do what we do more quickly. Exploring on a regular basis changes the nature of organizational change as well. We no longer have to work with with big deal, massive change. Instead, asking questions and making improvements becomes a new way of working that is expected and necessary and far less stressful on the organization itself.

We must put what we are expecting to happen out to the scrutiny of our exploration. We must invite the people in our organizations to push back on those expectations and assumptions and explore them without it making us anxious that things will grind to a halt. Those who created the systems and processes we are executing on (most often founders and senior leaders) must champion this exploring, not be uncomfortable about it. They need to be constantly asking if their once good idea is getting past its prime, not just standing in defense of it. Asking people to push back on what they have created or championed becomes a leadership requirement. Leaders have to demonstrate clearly that challenging and exploring is valuable to them. They need to lead with humility and publicly admit when they are no longer right, in order to get people who work for them to believe in exploring before executing.

You may have noted that in the last sentence I talked about leaders "no longer being right," not about them "being wrong." I believe that this is at the heart of much of our personal resistance to changing what we have created or championed in the past. We make the mistake of extrapolating the idea that if something is no longer right then that means it was always wrong. Now, you might say I am just engaging in semantics, but I would disagree. When we started doing it, most of what we executed on was the right or best way to get things done. Most of our systems and processes were intelligent and thorough in their design. But circumstances change, norms change, problems change, the world changes, and what was right becomes no longer right—no longer enough.

Systems and processes can be deeply believed as still being right long after they have proven by their results to no longer be so. Moreover, the systems built up around them can keep them alive like zombies in a horror film. Sadly, if a strong-enough minority of people believe in them, especially people with power, these systems can stick around and do great damage.

Executing in and of itself is not wrong, in fact it is necessary. It just requires exploring to keep it from ossifying and becoming no longer enough. Hanging on blindly to what has always worked is mighty dangerous in a world of innovation and disruption.

The five questions of Exploring Before Executing

Exploring Before Executing asks the five key questions below. All of them are phrased as a question you ask another individual or group. However, where you see "you" in the question, you might also want to consider putting "I" and asking yourself the questions as well. Not because you are the ultimate arbiter of the answers, but to uncover and say out loud what you hold to be true, what your current assumptions are. And I use the phrase "say out loud" specifically because the act of speaking something out loud often makes it more real and clearer than when it is swimming around the roiling seas of our minds. Try asking yourself some of these out loud and see if it feels different to you as you then answer yourself. If you're afraid to look foolish then you can just put your earbuds in, walk down the street and talk to yourself. No one will know the difference. Here are the questions, followed by an in-depth explanation of each.

Question 1. What do **you** think?

Question 2. What are you assuming is true?

Question 3. Whose voice is missing?

Question 4. What is your third-best idea?

Question 5. What didn't you say that needs saying?

1. What do **you** *think?*

This is the **curiosity-activation question**. It causes you to consider others' thinking first, before just moving ahead with the unspoken assumptions in your brain. Depending on your leadership style or interpersonal style, people may answer this question to a more or less truthful degree. If you keep asking it, and really show that you are listening, they will grow in their belief that you are truly curious and interested in what they think. One of the great follow-on questions for this, and nearly every other question in this book, is, "Tell me more." Just ask them to keep going until you really understand their view and the assumptions behind their view. "Tell me more," is non-confrontational and is why I prefer it over, "Why do you think that?" or "What makes you say that?" as those might imply that you hold a different view and that you are now looking for flaws in their think-ing, rather than to explore it with honest curiosity. If people believe you are listening, they will talk.

Next, ask yourself this same question, "What do I think?" and try to get out of your own head a little bit. Often, when asking myself this question, I say, "So, Michael, what do you think?" After which I answer as if there was someone questioning me who didn't live inside my head. I ask the clarifying questions I think another might ask. I definitely say, "Tell me more," until I think that I have said out loud what I am thinking. This can be an important tool too when talking with yourself—say it out loud. There is something that changes when we say things out loud that we are thinking, it makes them more real, we see them a little differently. So, get used to talking to yourself. In this case it doesn't make you crazy, it makes you smarter.

2. What are you assuming is true?

This is the **uncovering question**, and we need to ask the whole question when we use it. The key word here is not "assuming" or "true," it is *you* (or "we" if talking to a group). This is a question of curiosity for the whole group in the discussion. When talking to others, especially if you are a leader or influencer, it is important to emphasize the "you" or the "we" and that you understand that we might not all be assuming the same things. For this question, I like a white board (physical if in a room, digital when on video conference) where I can write down what everyone is saying in equal-size letters and with no differentiation between levels of hierarchy that may be present. Here I also leverage what Michael Bungay Stanier has called the best coaching question in the world (and he is probably right), "And what else?" The point of asking "What are we assuming is true?" is not to agree but to see the big picture of assumptions that form our thinking. It is to uncover that there are a lot of assumptions at play at all times and that we often ignore that fact. To be aware of your own assumptions you have to start by being aware that assumptions exist at all and that they are not just truth. Seeing a bunch of them on the white board starts to really bring that home and make us think, "Whoa, there's a lot of stuff here. What are the things that, if untrue or inaccurate, would really mess me/us up?"

3. Whose voice is missing?

This is the **echo-chamber question**. Recent research in sociology and communication has shown us that the internet has actually increased our likelihood of living in a world that reinforces beliefs we already have rather than making us think critically of ourselves. It turns out, sadly, that access to an overwhelming amount of information actually makes our thinking narrower. It is one of those counterintuitive realities that we need to remember as we try to learn and grow. So, asking this question allows the individual or group to consider how they might not bring enough diversity to the dialogue. Given that the vast majority of meetings seem to be driven by hierarchical level and not who is best suited to address the problems we are facing, this can be very useful to leaders. It gives a clear, group-led reason to start to diversify the thought in the group that will ultimately make decisions that matter. And, while you cannot have a cast of thousands weigh in on all discussions, it is more likely than not that an important voice is missing in nearly all of the discussions taking place.

4. What is your third-best idea?

This is the **keep-digging question**. I like it because it is a little irreverent and cheeky, and I like to think I am too. But it's not a silly question, it's precise. In asking people their ideas, over years of coaching and advising, there is a pattern that I have seen. Their first answer is simply the answer that causes them the least amount of discomfort and sounds most obviously right, often one that has been used before. However, it is rarely the best answer. Answer number two is generally a very cosmetically adjusted version of answer one, as they still haven't really thought about it. Answer three, however, is when you just cannot recycle that first answer again, it starts to sound silly coming out of your mouth. So, usually, people will pause and consider and give something thoughtful, different, and deeper. You can certainly go on and ask for fourth- and fifth-best ideas, and so on and so on. There are times when that is called for and useful. But often just leaping to "What is your third-best idea?" shortcuts the process and engages people in more creative thinking right off the bat. Of course, "Tell me more..." is a power move here as that might get you the fourth- or fifth-best idea (which is really the actual best idea) or it may allow you to dive deeper into this more creative "third-best" idea and see where that takes you.

5. What didn't you say that needs saying?

This is the **go-where-the-fear-is question** and is the most introspective, and potentially confrontational, of them all. It implies, first off, that we might not be saying everything. If that is so, then there is something preventing us, getting in the way, or scaring us off. And, if you are the leader in the discussion with a group, it might just be you. So, start with yourself. "What didn't I say that needs saying?" is the place to start. Oh, and you need to answer the question too. Right there, in front of people, in as unguarded a way as possible. Spend that moment to not know, to be introspective, and to let the team see you being vulnerable enough to ask and answer the question. Lead out loud and make it okay for others to do the same. People follow what leaders do, not what they say. That old trope is as timeworn as it is ignored in the reality of organizational life—and it is still true nonetheless.

When asking myself this question I often take it a little further and ask myself, "Where is the fear for me in this question? What don't I want to say out loud (because acknowledging it scares me for some reason)?" If you want to truly know yourself and accelerate your own personal growth and change, honestly looking at what you fear and then going there is potentially one of the most freeing things you can do. More often than not, fear is telling us what we need to do and where we need to go, as odd as that may sound.

Finally, if you want to empower your team further here, give them explicit permission to answer the bonus question, "What question didn't I ask you, that I should have?"

Curiosity is at the heart of transformation

Curiosity is an aspect of every single capability in this book. Let me link it to our six capabilities this way:

1 Curiosity about what we think we know leads to Exploring
2 Curiosity about what we don't know leads to Learning
3 Curiosity about how we can be different leads to Changing

4 Curiosity about the way to get there leads to Pathfinding

5 Curiosity about what might be possible leads to Innovating

6 Curiosity about others leads to Humanizing

Curiosity is the fundamental core of a set of skills that underlies everything in this book. It is the spiritual parent of everything here. We will use it as we define every one of these capabilities, talk about how to act on them, and talk about how to learn from those actions, for individuals and across global organizations and networks.

Exploring is about getting actively and systematically curious about what we think we know. As humans, we need to figure things out. We find security in looking for that pattern or framework of assumptions and beliefs in the world around us so we can move forward "knowing" what is happening. Having the security of this framework prevents us from having to think much more about it. And why would we? It's not as if our brains are actually the blank slates that we think they are. They are not neutral observers that weed out what is true from what is false and then give us the one true picture of reality. But we certainly think they are!

It is a human phenomenon that nearly every single developed person on the planet believes that, for the most part, they are the ones who see the world clearly. They are the ones who know truth. Yet what they call truth can diverge wildly from what another calls truth. All they know is that the other person is misled, mistaken, misspeaking, misleading, or just plain stupid.

As I said earlier, I am not a neuroscientist and I am not going to attempt to explain the biological science that elucidates how neural pathways and neural networks evolved and form. But I will share a scientific fact and a metaphor that has been used by noted neurologists in the past. What we think of as "thinking" happens in our neural pathways and neural networks. When we "learn" something, it means that we have effectively put in place a neural network that can be reactivated at need. Here's the metaphor: the neural networks in our brain are like a riverbed. While the initial flow (in this case of thought, not water) might be a bit random and dictated by our experiences and context, over time the channels get more pronounced and the water that is information tends to mostly stay to those channels. Over time, our thought will follow this path of least resistance until it becomes a part of us. Until it becomes truth. And it is very hard to change the course of that river. Very hard.

In countless experiments and research about the brain and beliefs, we find that not only is it nearly impossible for others to "change our mind" but that we tend to come away from those interactions that confront our beliefs—our truth—with an even deeper-held belief that we started with, or we even go further into that belief. When confronted with others who do not share our beliefs, we often end up becoming more extreme in those beliefs.[3]

As we discussed earlier, changing our minds is very difficult. But there are some brilliant people trying to put together ways to solve this problem. One of the simplest, and yet one of the best, I know of comes from the amazing work of Robert Kegan and Lisa Laskow Lahey at Harvard University's Graduate School of Education.[4] The foundation of their model concerns individuals going through a process to find their hidden or unspoken assumptions (those river-beds we talked about) and then to perform small, recoverable tests to see if those assumptions hold water. If, over time, we find some fault with our own assumptions, and we keep finding those faults, then we can change the course and change our minds.

You can probably see where this is going. I have stated that exploring is something we have to value before executing. Not that executing is wrong, it just is not enough and it is not where we should start. So, I am asking you to believe that exploring is better or necessary before we execute. That is a belief, an assumption—one of six—on which this book is based. But you might believe differently. And if you are one of those people reading this book who find yourself disagreeing with me, I don't think I can change your mind and I won't try. But I will ask you if you think it just might be worth being a little more curious and pausing your very active brain flow? Might there be some value in considering the possibility? If so, here's what I want you to do.

Tools for transformation—operationalizing your curiosity

What do the curious do? They ask questions. Questions are how we activate, how we operationalize, curiosity. For each of these six chapters on the new capabilities that create a heart of transformation, I have given you some questions you can ask, of yourself and others.

My simple formula in using these questions—five of which you have already seen—is the four As: **Allow, Ask, Assess,** and **Again.**

THE FOUR As

- **Allow**. Say to yourself, "You know, it's worth it to find out if there's anything to this stuff at all. I'll allow the possibility and, even if I doubt it, it's worth asking the question."

- **Ask**. Use the questions in the ways they are suggested—and when you use one of them, don't just do it once. Do it at least three times, but with your whole heart (more about that in a moment).

- **Assess**. Pause again and debrief yourself to try to determine what just happened. Did you get the answer or response that fits what you believe, or did what happen not quite fit with your expectations—your assumptions?

- **Again**. If your assumptions are being challenged then keep up the cycle of curiosity until you start to feel a little more certain (either in your old beliefs or the new). Just remain in that curious place by asking good questions and see what happens.

That's it. That's what we are going to do—**Allow, Ask, Assess,** and **Again.** In each of the ensuing five chapters you will find questions like the ones you found above. Follow the formula and keep learning and growing. Oh, and one final thing. If you can follow the four As with someone else, it is even more powerful. You don't have to do it on your own.

Making it real—three times with your whole heart

Earlier I said that I want you to ask these questions "three times, with your whole heart." Let me explain what I mean. There are a lot of ways to ask a question. But I am certain you have all had the experience of being asked a question (and maybe doing the asking) where you knew that the person asking was not sincere or really did not care. Whatever the reason, we have all been asked questions insincerely, and we do not like it. It feels worse than just being discounted, disregarded, or ignored. If what you think doesn't really matter, then someone pretending like it does just adds insult to injury and frustration to the relationship.

Above, I said you need to start by *Allowing* the possibility before you *Ask* and *Assess*. That is what **Three Times with Your Whole Heart** is about; allowing that the question is worth asking. And if it is worth asking, it is worth listening to the answer. So, ask the question with as much true curiosity as you can and try to suspend any biases, assumptions, or answers of your own that you have at the ready. Set them aside and enter a momentary world of a blank slate where anything is possible, and really listen to what you hear. And then do it *Again*.

You might need to pause and take a breath to get ready to do this. It's not as easy as it sounds. Furthermore, don't ask these questions just once. You need to get more data, more practice. *Do it at least three times*. This gives you a meaningful set of experiences. Small, yes, but still meaningful. And you will probably just be getting passable at really being wholeheartedly curious by the third time you ask it. If you follow the **Three Times with Your Whole Heart** guideline you will find the potential for discovery and learning, using any of the questions in this book, to be much greater. Remember, using your whole heart is the best way to accelerate building your heart of transformation.

Endnotes

1 Gryta, T and Mann, T (2020) *Lights Out: Pride, delusion, and the fall of General Electric*, Houghton Mifflin Harcourt, Boston
2 Ibid
3 For further reading check out: Shermer, M (2012) *The Believing Brain: From ghosts and gods to politics and conspiracies—how we construct beliefs and reinforce them as truths*, St Martin's Griffin, New York
4 Kegan, R and Laskow Lahey, L (2009) *Immunity to Change: How to overcome it and unlock potential in yourself and your organization*, Harvard Business School, Boston

05

Learning Before Knowing

A story of learning

Early in 2017, on a slushy and cold day, I found myself in Cambridge, Massachusetts sitting next to Clayton Christensen. I only have a few heroes in my life and Clay Christensen is one of them. When he passed in early 2020, we lost a great thinker but, more importantly, a deeply humane human being. Clay had a spirit of humility and self-awareness that was truly wonderful, especially for a man who could easily lay claim to so many accolades and much praise had he chosen to do so. The fact that he did not was, I think, because he knew how doing so prods one down the slippery slope of our own over-developed egos and fosters a false sense of knowing more than we actually know.

I was introduced to Clay by Bob Moesta. Bob would also make my hero list for a number of reasons, and I am honored to call him a friend. We will touch on Bob again later in this book. But the story I want to relate to you now is about Clay and how he helped put into context and words for me something very profound about Learning Before Knowing, the subject of this chapter and the capability up next.

In this book I am talking about transformation, and the digital disruption and need for innovation that presages it, and Clay literally wrote the book on Innovation. *The Innovator's Dilemma* is a foundational book on just how deeply difficult it is to disrupt ourselves and let go of our own great solutions that have outlived their usefulness now that the problem they once so elegantly or effectively solved has changed or gone away.

The conversation that wintry day was a free-ranging exchange of ideas with no agenda or outcome, it was a place to think together. I had brought along a colleague from GE and there was also a professor and venture capitalist from another lauded university with us that day. And it was, as I said, a day of free exchange of ideas where Clay was simply a part of the thinking. He did not lead it, nor did we all sit in hushed silence listening to the master (although I gladly would have). Instead we talked together as colleagues, peers, and nascent friends brought together by old friends and new ideas. It was without doubt a highlight in my career.

At one point, we were discussing organizations and leaders and how they were having such difficulty changing the way they led to suit a more digital and agile world. During a pause in the discussion Clay said, "Michael, I'm having a bit of an epiphany here." And, yes, at this point, the room did go silent. He continued, "It used to be that we needed to have developed the skills in order to get the job. Now we have the job but we need to develop the skills to do it!" We went on to talk about how disorienting this is and how difficult it can be to accept, especially when that job was something that gave its holder status, power, wealth, etc., and was something they felt they deserved because of their hard work and **what they knew**. They deserved the rewards, because they knew the most and were, therefore, more valuable and best positioned to lead others. Moreover, if they no longer knew all that they needed to do the job it threatened their sense of legitimacy in their roles, and this was intolerably destabilizing for most.

Nonetheless, this new "digital" world was challenging all of our knowledge. If seemed as if young kids in jeans and flip-flops were building game-changing organizations seemingly overnight. Disruption was everywhere and businesses were flailing while trying to adapt or failing to see the need to adapt.

Lots has already been written on digital disruption, that is not our focus here. Our focus here is the heart of Clay's epiphany—the need to move from seeing value as based on knowing to realizing that value is based on learning. I have heard it said that we are moving from the age of the knowledge worker to the age of the learning worker. This is what Clay was referring to in that moment. What sticks with me the most is that he was having this realization for himself, it was not just a lesson for everyone else. He was not passing on his knowledge, he was learning this as we spoke. A man of great knowledge—a Harvard Business School professor who achieved the rank of full professor faster than anyone to come before him, a Rhodes Scholar, a bestselling author, a board member and advisor to the world's most successful companies, a man whose knowledge was astounding—was processing and verbalizing this lesson: that learning mattered more.

His humility, vulnerability, and desire to learn, and be seen learning, despite all the reasons one might say he did not need to, will never leave me and I will endeavor to continue to remember and learn from the gift of that lesson for the rest of my life. It is a gift he gave me that truly keeps on giving.

The journey from labor to knowledge to learning

At the beginning of this book, we looked at the link between the rise of land ownership and the beginnings of the modern organization. For the next evolutionary step in the history of organizations, we need to look at what changed in the Industrial Revolution. With the advent of production, and more specifically, the production line, working lives went through another major shift. You were no longer a farmer or craftsperson who made your own way and depended only on your family, and maybe a partner or two, for producing, selling, and making a living. Now we were building factories that employed others. The shift from *my* business to *the* business had begun.

While the autonomy of the worker was lessened, so was their risk. Overall and over time, the ability of the average person to get hired for a job, stay employed, have a predictable income, and begin to move out of subsistence living into a standard of living, was being realized. Certainly, in the early days the pay was not much, and that standard was low. There were also almost no safety nets, and a lot of other challenges that could bring economic hardship and loss. But, nonetheless, the factory worker began to gain a foothold in a world where they had before been servants and have-nots.

Labor had value. As labor became the key to the success of a business, those who labored began to see their value in the economy and the power began to shift. Subtly, yes, and slowly, but it did move. The people who made up the labor class began to organize. Unions were formed, often through bloody and violent conflict. But, in the end, without a means of production there was no production, so the laborer began to develop a stronger place in working society with increasing standards of living. People began to develop expectations. If they learned a skill, it had value. If they increased in that skill or developed others, they had more value. Over the years, a new class of people emerged—a middle class.

That is decades and decades of history shoved into a paragraph or two, but you get the idea. Workers became the major means of production. Some of them were needed to direct or oversee other workers and the management class was born as well. The working world settled into a successful pattern that created, particularly in the United States, a robust and thriving economy—the realization of the "American Dream" for so many. It is also true that war and other factors played a part in the shifting tides of work and economic success. However, it was largely a move to labor and production that gave us the modern economy of the 1900s and the rise of the labor middle class, as well as the rise of some as a burgeoning management class. They reaped the rewards of being considered the best of the laborers who had the skills and knowledge to lead the other laborers. Whether that was based entirely on merit or also on factors of class, gender, and race is the subject for another book.

But, regardless of how meritocracy-based the management roles were, something interesting was inexorably happening to the workforce in general. As laborers grew in skills, the machines grew in sophistication. Automation began to take away the tasks that required less knowledge and skill, making way for the laborer to learn and perform tasks that were less repetitive and required more thought, not just motion. As our tools and technologies evolved, so did our ability to use them and to invent them. The more we knew about the means of production, and the possibilities untried, the more we could improve those means of production and extract more value from the labor of the worker. Margins went up, wages went up, standards of living went up. Things continued to move forward, and the value of mere labor began to yield to the value of skilled labor and then knowledge.

Over time, the perks of being in the management class also became clearer. I think of the movie *EDtv* (1999), where Rob Reiner's network boss character says to Ellen DeGeneres's producer character, "And you know how I know I'm right? Because I'm driving the big car and you're driving the little car." But despite the big car versus little car disparities that developed, the means of success were the same—the ability to leverage labor as a means of production and the knowledge of how to support the output of that labor with better and better technologies.

The term "knowledge worker" began to appear in the late 1950s and is mostly associated with the work of an early guru of management theory and corporate practices, Peter Drucker. It is unclear that Drucker invented the term, but he certainly popularized it. For Drucker, the knowledge worker was marked by the fact that their primary value resided in what they knew, not what they did. Examples were programmers, physicians, engineers, lawyers, and many other white-collar workers whose line of work required them to "think for a living."

A tale that illustrates the value of the knowledge worker is as follows. A company had invested in a new machine to greatly increase production and profitability, but it broke. They could not fix it and so they called in an expert from the company that had made the machine. He came out, looked at it for a few moments and then went into his bag, brought out a small screwdriver and, from among the myriad screws, levers, knobs, and gauges, tightened one screw on a valve. The machine was restarted and roared to life flawlessly. The expert then handed the owner of the company a bill for US $1,000. The owner looked at him incredulously and said, "This is outrageous! How in the world is it possible to justify a $1,000 bill for turning a screw!" "Oh," the expert replied, "the cost of turning the screw was only $5." "Well then why is this bill for $1,000?" asked the now befuddled owner. The expert replied, "It's $5 for turning the screw and $995 for knowing which screw to turn."

The knowledge worker was born.

And the knowledge worker has risen and matured. The vast fortunes of the latter years of the 20th century and the beginnings of the 21st century have nearly all been due to the creation and innovation of the knowledge worker, particularly the technology knowledge worker. Digital technologies have created an entirely new class of the super-rich, as well as the merely really rich, based on stock valuations skyrocketing from the disruption and reinvention (or invention) of entire industries. We have just about perfected the value of the knowledge worker, at least if perfected means that they are the most economically successful and wealthy with the most opportunity to achieve and grow wealth. In fact, we have become so good at exploiting and leveraging knowledge work that something insidious has begun to happen. The gains of the middle class brought about by moving from industrial work into knowledge work have begun to be pulled back. Income disparity is on the rise. The rich are richer than ever before, year after year, and those at the lower end of the economy are losing ground on income, opportunity, and savings annually.

Just a note, I am using class here to denote a group classification built on rough socio-economic factors—it is in no way related to more entrenched social classes found in some societies. It also assumes that you can move from class to class by means of socio-economic gains and that class is not fixed at birth. Although, admittedly, those socio-economic gains can be hard to come by.

You don't need this book to see the impact on our societies of these growing inequities. They have been felt especially acutely in the United States, as have their impact on a middle class that finds itself losing ground yearly and on a lower socio-economic class that is getting more and more desperate. I retell these tales not to make a political or socio-economical statement, but to provide background for the change that we are now on the precipice of—the change from the knowledge worker to the learning worker. Because something else interesting has happened and the knowledge workers may just have hoisted themselves on their own petards.

The knowledge workers of the 20th century brought with their rise an exponential growth in technology—digital information technology being the most prominent with its overwhelmingly enormous impact on, well, nearly everything. With that growth came more growth. Industries that had done virtually the same things for decades now found themselves considered luddites and their entire markets had apparently abandoned them in what felt like an overnight timeframe. And then the disruptors were disrupted by someone else. Occasionally they were disrupted by themselves. It appears to be the companies that are the ones that continue to thrive and grow that will happily trash today what was their brilliant innovation of yesterday in order to bank on their ability to build (or monetize) tomorrow faster than their competitors. While different consulting models of organizational strategy have always paid lip service to having an investment in innovation for the future, it was rarely what kept CEOs up at night and was often the first thing to be cut when the quarterly reporting demanded 0.1 percent more cost savings to meet the projected numbers, which we made up in the first place. (Do I sound cynical about the short-term thinking of the modern stock-price-driven financial models that dominate corporate thinking despite some recent talk of changing that? Good, I am!)

Innovation was, for most, an expendable nice-to-have. The idea that it is when you are at the top of your cash-producing game that you should look to completely reinvent what is working today was anathema to comfortable corporate leaders who were overseeing execution of the old tried and true. It was simply too much of a mental leap to see that what was once the very successful answer now no longer was. Giving up what appeared to be sure success for speculative new success was frightening and considered too risky. We are creatures that long for certainty and safety, at an evolutionary biological level. Sometimes we even make up things that make us feel good and safe like, "And why should tomorrow be any different?" But it will be.

I previously quoted a friend and teacher of mine who gave me the phrase that we are "living in a world of fifth-generation information technology and second-generation human systems." I love what that sentence says. It so clearly encapsulates the problem of nearly unfettered technology growth and its impact on human systems—human systems that are largely unchanged in their hierarchical structures, ways of measuring value, focus on roles over people, etc. I think at the heart of this disparity between technology and people sits learning.

How technology advances demand human advances

The world of software development gave us many gifts. One of them is the thinking that produced Agile. Now, I am not a coder and have not developed software through the Agile mindset or using any other similar approach (aside from some fairly sad attempts at HTML on my early website). But I know enough about it and things like Lean, Design Thinking, etc., to understand that one of the key components of its success is the ability of the technologists to learn. They had to get data, interpret what it could mean, adjust (or pivot), see if they were right or wrong, and then iteratively continue until they learned what they needed to know to produce a superior product that people wanted to buy and that they could build and sell.

It begins with the first of four fundamentals of Agile, "Individuals and interactions over processes and tools."[1] On the web page for the Agile manifesto they even reduce the font of "Processes and Tools" to reinforce the point. The implication is clear, this is a human-driven system, not a process-driven one. The process serves the people, not the other way around. This is important and we will come back to this again throughout this book. The process serves the people—this is fundamentally different from where we started in the Industrial Revolution.

This statement is bookended with the last of the 12 principles of Agile, "At regular intervals, the team reflects on how to become more effective, then tunes and **adjusts its behavior accordingly**." They learn.

Look at the bottom-line message that this sandwich of phrases produces—people get together and look at how they interact with each other so they can learn to work together better. By doing so, our technology knowledge workers created a learning environment in which they were able to greatly accelerate their own evolution, leap-frogging the incumbent companies which had grown complacent, and bringing their massive disruptions to the economy. The technologies improve faster and faster, capabilities grow, and innovations like AI and machine learning continue to advance what technology can do and how work can be done. Technologies that themselves can learn are pushing growth and development. The outcome is more than just the creation of new solutions—it is the creation of new problems.

The other outcome is that we are able to use the massive amounts of data we can now crunch to solve incredibly large and complex problems, problems beyond our ability to solve without technology. This in turn means that we need to disrupt and innovate on ourselves faster than ever.

In *Humility is the New Smart* (2017), Ed Hess and Katherine Ludwig have said that "what we know to be true now has a shelf-life of about three years."[2] In this new reality, the value of knowledge is plummeting and the ability to unlearn what you know to be true so you can learn what is now "true" is where the ability to advance and grow lies. Our knowledge workers have created a technological juggernaut that has outpaced the organizations they exist in or serve. Now we have to make the pivot from knowing to learning and we have to make it quickly. How to do that is what we are going to discuss next in this chapter.

Before I go into the learning worker, I would like to address another way I have heard the new value of this emerging type of worker expressed: the relationship worker. I first heard this term for the new value worker from Geoff Colvin when reading *Humans are Underrated*.[3] This is the worker he sees replacing the knowledge worker. I have chosen to use learning worker because I think it captures the essence of the relationship worker but also expands on it in a meaningful way.

The idea behind a relationship worker is that it is this kind of worker who can form the best teams. In a world where the problems are changing so rapidly and becoming more complex, a team is required to find and solve problems, no one person is up to the task. It now takes a village. And I agree with Colvin that the ability to build relationships and teams is critical in this world of a new excellence. However, how do we become great team builders? How do we inspire and rally people to focus on the greater goal instead of just their personal goals? How do we navigate all the emotional and relational issues of teams? By learning. Learning about each and every person on the team. We must understand what makes them tick—what are their hopes and dreams, their personal situations and aspirations, what are they good at and what do they want to get better at? We will go further into this, and how to do it, when we discuss Humanizing Before Organizing later in the book.

The learning worker also has one very crucial individual that they have to be sure to learn all about. A being who is slippery, who tells them subtle lies, who resists being questioned. Themselves.

As you go through this book, you will see that much of it boils down to developing the self-awareness we all need to then build our awareness of others so that we can make better choices together. A heart of transformation beats in your own chest first.

Learning to learn

So how do I learn to learn? I mean, I've been learning all my life, haven't I? These are good questions, and obvious ones. The thing with learning is that what you have learned, your acquired knowledge, accumulates and turns into knowing. When I champion Learning Before Knowing, I am not saying knowing nothing is the goal. Obviously, knowledge is good, just ask Emil Faber. It helps you communicate. It helps you add value and move things forward. It helps you win at quiz nights in the local pub. But the knowledge that concerns me is not the collection of facts and information that you have gained over the years. These are good (mostly) and allow you to figure things out. For example, since you know how to drive a car and read a map or follow a GPS, you can figure out how to drive to someplace you have never been to before and probably not get lost. You know how to read gauges and do math so you can probably manage to not run out of fuel (or charge if you've gone electric). You know what can happen when you drive erratically or too fast and so you will probably get where you are going safely. All of that requires knowledge you have learned over your life—some of it general and some of it specific to the task. And you know that you know these things.

No, what I am concerned about are the things that you know but that you are less cognizant of, something we broached in Chapter 4—your assumptions. Actually, maybe operating assumptions is a more precise way to say it. There are two things to look at here. The first are things you have come to "know" through learned experience or social constructions. The second are the things you "know" because that is just how your brain works. Knowledge is made up of so many things, some that we are aware of and some that we are not. Some we can readily add to, or change, and some prove to be devilishly intractable.

Why my truth is truer than yours

Let's start with what we have come to know. We all have a set of beliefs or values that we have come to expect as true. It is indeed fascinating that so many people **absolutely know** so many things to be absolutely true and yet there are millions of other people who **absolutely know** that the opposite or something completely incompatible is absolutely true. I don't think I have to spend much time here. Look at religion. Which god is the one true god? Or is there one true god? Civilizations rise and fall on beliefs in a higher power and the disparity between which power is the real one or if there is a higher power at all. In the face of so much disagreement, sometimes vehement and violent disagreement, how can we all be so sure of what we know?

Humans are social. There is good evidence for the fact that we evolved to be social because humans in groups and tribes had more success just surviving. (Of course, you would have to know that evolution was true to believe that but let's just assume, for the sake of this section, that we are a species that evolves.) Part of being social creatures is finding the commonalities that bind our societies, of whatever size, together. From early days we learn from our parents, and the other influences in our society, what is true. Right and wrong, good and bad; these are all things that we come to share. Why, because they keep us together, they keep the tribe strong. And the strong tribe is... well, strong. The group, organization, or society can do more together than individually if its members are aligned in their beliefs and working together toward shared goals.

Further, we hold each other accountable and judge whether or not we demonstrate evidence that we share the beliefs that make us a part of the tribe. Those who do not adhere can be ejected from the tribe and have to find a new one or go out on their own, and I am not talking cave dwellers here—this is what happens every day. It is one of the reasons we will adhere to cultural norms that we actually think are ineffective or even damaging. Many times, we would rather be a part of something broken than on our own and whole.

I will never forget an experience with one organization where I found myself shocked by their norms. One was in regard to rewards and recognition. I was told that it really didn't matter what results or business outcomes I produced or effected, what mattered was who I knew (especially those in power) and what they said about me. Did they like me or not? That was what mattered. That would determine rewards, recognition, mobility, and even longevity (or not, as we shall see). And I am not going back and embellishing. This message about what mattered, I have related almost verbatim as it was something that struck me so hard at the time as to be as unforgettable as the brain allows. But what really challenged me was when I asked that person what they thought about this organizational cultural reality. They acknowledged that this was not necessarily a good aspect of the company, in fact it was downright bad. However, their belief was that changing that organizational reality was just not possible, so it was best just to embrace it and start making friends and figuring out what the people with power and influence wanted to hear. At least if I wanted to stay there and be successful. I guess you could say this was practical and would be the right guidance if I desired to continue to work with that organization, but that was something that I now no longer wanted to do. I was miserable with this. But, even then, did I run for the door immediately? No, I tried to accommodate and adapt and justify because I didn't want to *not* belong. Part of me began to question my own convictions. I was the odd man out, maybe I was wrong here? After all, the rest of the tribe seemed to be doing just fine with this norm. And so, I tried extremely hard to be a part of something that I absolutely didn't want to be a part of anymore. But I didn't like it, and I could not hide that. I'm a good guy to play poker with, I tend to wear my heart on my sleeve. And my apparent unhappiness with this cultural norm was what caused the culture to eventually reject me anyway. If you were to talk to many of the people involved, good people, mind you, I think that they would say the issue resided in my being unable to adapt to the way of that organization, not that the organization's way was fundamentally corrupted. Those who are no longer there might have a different view. But we tend to believe that you can't argue with success—and the company is very successful, and the people in it are very successful. So, it works, right?

Looking back, I can see I was seduced by a desire to be included (or maybe a fear or shame of being excluded). We stand by our tribe; we stand by what we are taught is true and works. We might see some cracks appear here and there, but we can easily paper those over for the benefit of being secure in what we know and, more importantly, so we can belong.

Then, there is what happens at a more fundamental level in our brains.

The truth that saves us can also derail us

I am going to continue to flirt with the role of amateur neuroscientist for a bit and talk a little about how the brain works; the three major parts of it and how they engage with what we know. Bear with me as this has some fascinating implications for Learning Before Knowing.

Let's start with the triune brain. Neuroscientist Paul D MacLean first wrote about this in 1960. He described a brain in three parts— the reptilian complex (or lizard brain located in the brain stem), the limbic system, and the neocortex. While this model is oversimplified, and some of the details of its evolutionary theory shown to be wrong, it remains one of the most useful models for understanding the brain, especially from a human behavior perspective.[4] Remember our friend George Box from way back at the start of this book? Here is another model that is "wrong, but useful." Here's how it works.

Our newest brain is the neocortex. It is also the biggest of our brains, the one that we think we think with. In the neocortex we have language, mathematics, abstraction, perception, etc. When we talk about thinking, generally it is about this rational and logical brain that we are referring to when we do. It is by far the biggest part of the brain physically and requires far more energy than the other two parts of the brain to function. When you start to cut off its oxygenated blood supply, it starts to falter and fail. If you do that for too long you become unconscious or go into a coma. However, you can survive, often for decades, with this brain weak or dead.

Next is the limbic system. If the neocortex is our thinking brain, the limbic brain is, at it's very simplest, our emotional brain. It is concerned with, "Do I like you?" "Do you like me?" "Are we a part of the same tribe or not?" Emotion, parental and reproductive behavior, as well as other relationship behavior, comes primarily from this brain. When we feel that warm rush of affection for someone it is often because of what is happening in the limbic system. This brain takes less energy to run than the neocortex and is older in its evolution. Like the neocortex, this brain can cease to actively function while we remain alive. We will have no consciousness or quality of life, perhaps, but we can remain alive.

Finally, we have the R-complex or the lizard brain, our instinctual brain. This is the tiny granddaddy of them all. It formed first, and it was not concerned with the matters of the heart or thinking deep thoughts, like the limbic system and neocortex, respectively. No, the lizard was there to survive, to keep us alive. Humans have an instinct to live, driven by the reptilian brain—an instinct that is strong and that influences us constantly without our ever becoming cognizant of it. It also is core to keeping our heart beating and other autonomic functions functioning. If this brain ceases to live, then so do we. It's game over. And, so, it plays a conservative game to protect itself. It does this by being a true and constant pessimist.[5]

When new stimuli come into the purview of the brains, it is the lizard brain that jumps on it the fastest. It has a nanoseconds survival screen it deploys in which to do this and that goes something like this:

> Are you clearly my enemy, a threat to me and my resources? If so, I will react accordingly—freeze, fight, flight, or play dead. If not, are you a potential mate for me, to carry on my genes? If so, swipe right. If not, are you a known or perceived friend to me, someone who adds to me or my resources? If yes, I welcome you with open arms. If you are clearly none of the above, then I can be indifferent to you and move on to the next thing.

Finally, if there is insufficient information to categorize you into friend, potential sexual partner, enemy, or person deserving indifference, then the lizard defaults to the negative and puts you into enemy territory. Better to assume a defensive position than let an unmarked enemy get close enough to threaten our survival. The reptilian brain makes these judgments before the other brains can get around to all of that feeling and thinking stuff—it doesn't have the luxury of time; our very survival is at stake. Or at least that is how it has evolved to see the world around us.

If you want to see this happening in action in your own life, just think of taking a stroll down a busy sidewalk in a city somewhere. You might have a few reactions to the myriad people also strolling by. You might find one threatening and feel the quickening of pulse as you pause and get ready for fight, flight, or hoping they pass you by.

You may find another person quite attractive and feel that happy rush of chemicals that goes to your brain but seems to reside in your stomach in the form of butterflies. You might also feel the happiness from the recognition of a good friend and wave that person over. But, mostly, you will pay no attention to them, other than not to collide with them, and they will be forever out of your mind. They are lost to indifference as you go about your merry way. (Of course, the COVID-19 pandemic raised the threat level of strangers significantly to the point where we definitely felt less indifference on a crowded city street than we used to do.)

Why does this little lesson in the brain matter to us when it comes to Learning Before Knowing? Because it begins to show us that what we "know" actually comes from some fairly interesting, probably questionable, places and that it is not simply founded in rationality or logic but is something much deeper and difficult to see. We started by discussing things we came to know through nurture or societal constructs and cultures; things that might not be true, but that serve the purposes of keeping the tribe together and fostering belonging. Now we see that other things that we know can come from unconscious places driven by reactions that have evolved to protect us, but not necessarily show us what is true or react in proportion to the actual threat or risk.

Our other brains, even the big thinking one, are complicit as well. The fundamental attribution error is a theory that posits that we have a tendency to underemphasize situational explanations for another individual's observed behavior while overemphasizing dispositional and personality-based explanations for their behavior. This effect has been described as the tendency to believe that what people do reflects who they are. Oh, and we tend to think the opposite about ourselves. In other words, when another person does something "wrong," it is basically character flaw. When we do something ourselves that another person apparently considers "wrong" it was the situation that caused it; we are really not to blame here. This is something that our brain just knows. There are different theories as to why our brains process things this way, but most agree that the behavior predominates, regardless of its etymology. Some refer to this as correspondence bias or attribution effect, but the outcome is the same.

We also fall prey to confirmation bias. This one is the tendency for us to search for, interpret, favor, and recall information that confirms or supports beliefs or values we already hold. This shows up in the search for information where our brains subconsciously cherry-pick the things that support what we already "know," or they interpret things to support what we already "know," and they actually remember things in such a way as to support what we already "know," whether that was what actually happened or not!

The research on this is fascinating and, if you know that this is a bunch of nonsense and that your brain is always rational, fair, and accurate, then I suggest you dig into the truly disorienting field of how unreliable our own minds, and pictures of reality, actually are. Or not... if you still think you're probably right.

I share all of this stuff not just because it is interesting and it is something we should understand, but because it illustrates so clearly how hard it is to "un-know" something. In many cases, if not most, for us to learn something new we have to unlearn something old. There are many reasons for feeling good about what we think we know: it used to be right (and, yes, it likely did); the cost of it not being right is high (subconsciously, it's existential); and our brain works overtime to convince us it is right. But too often, what we "know" is no longer right or true, if it ever was.

David Foster Wallace captures this so eloquently in his essay "This is Water":[6]

> Here is just one example of the total wrongness of something I tend to be automatically sure of: everything in my own immediate experience supports my deep belief that I am the absolute center of the universe; the realest, most vivid and important person in existence. We rarely think about this sort of natural, basic self-centeredness because it's so socially repulsive. But it's pretty much the same for all of us. It is our default setting, hard-wired into our boards at birth. Think about it: there is no experience you have had that you are not the absolute center of.

The five questions of Learning Before Knowing

So, now that we know that we might not know what we know we know, or now that we are willing to entertain the possibility, what do we do? We need to have tools to allow us to look at our assumptions—what we know—and challenge them. So, it is back to our old friend, the question, and back to the formula of: **Allow, Ask, Assess,** and **Again**. In Exploring Before Executing, we first posited our questions as questions for others and then looked at how we ask them of ourselves. This time, we will do the opposite because *knowing* is so intrinsic that it is hard to help others until we have helped ourselves. Nonetheless, each of these questions can be, and should be, asked of others, once you have earned the right to do so. Here are the five questions of Learning Before Knowing.

Question 1: Who challenges my beliefs?
Question 2: How is my idea wrong?
Question 3: What is my blind spot?
Question 4: When was the last time I was wrong?
Question 5: Am I okay with not knowing?

---

1. Who challenges my beliefs?

This is the **healthy self-doubt question**. We all need people who love us enough to tell us when we are full of (you insert your favorite excretory term here). A friend and mentor once said to me that, "The higher you go in an organization, the harder it is to find anyone to tell you the truth." If you are going to have people who challenge your beliefs in your life, then there are three specific things you absolutely must do. The first is to seek them out actively. You have to look for people who you think have the character and the insight to give you a different perspective and make you think about whether what you "know" or not is true. Second, you have to invite them in and give them explicit permission to do so. You must cultivate these people and ask them, even beg them, for the unvarnished truth as they see it.

Remember, you don't have to see it their way or do what they advise. But you need the information so you can thoughtfully consider and come to your own conclusions. If you are a leader, I can guarantee there are people out there who work under you that see you clearly, but do not feel welcome to tell you what they see. Third, you must show your gratitude. Do this privately and do this publicly. A leader who shares their stories of being wrong, and publicly thanks the people who helped them see this, will find that more and more people will start to feel safe to be honest and open with them.

2. How is my idea wrong?

This is the **question that acknowledges your fallibility**. Notice that this question is not "Is my idea wrong?" That question assumes it might not be. The response, "Hey Boss, sounds good to me!" is the comforting lie of expedience that can trip us up badly. No, we need to put out there that there is a good chance something is wrong, even if a small something, with our idea, position, or (most importantly) belief. When I ask this question of a reluctant group, mostly because I am the boss, I sometimes have to push it a bit further when they do not find anything and ask them, "Okay, but if there was something wrong, what would it be?" and keep pushing for that small something that opens up a whole new way of seeing things. Don't be satisfied until you are satisfied. If you never feel any momentary pain, embarrassment, or momentary shame then you are probably not getting quality feedback or answers. The brief moments and short-lived discomfort required of us to be challenged on what we "know" will be paid back in multiples when we learn something new and, more critically, get better at learning how to learn.

3. What is my blind spot?

This is the **problematic-patterns question**. While similar to "How is my idea wrong?" this question starts to help us look at patterns of error in our assumptions. The blind spot is a good metaphor. All of us who have driven a vehicle have likely had that moment of panic when we realized that something was happening just outside our vehicle that we were utterly oblivious to, but that could have had devastating consequences. It is a shock to suddenly have the reality you are living in altered not by introducing something new but by your just finally noticing it. It's a funny thing about blind spots. If you and I share them then we will probably exacerbate each other's situation. Talking to people around you and asking them to give you feedback on this question is a longitudinal study. See what the answers are, look for the connections. Some will be obvious, others will not. Many people will answer this question with some vagueness that is meant to be kindness. But if we ask enough people, then even through the mist of niceness we will start to see the rocks that our ship of assumptions will likely falter on unless we change course.

4. When was the last time I was wrong?

This is the **reality-check question** that tells you how well the other questions have been answered (or asked). If the answer is "a long time ago" then you are probably already in trouble. Because it wasn't that long ago at all that you were wrong about something, you just don't realize that, and that is a dangerous place to be. If your team has a hard time answering this question, then you had better be wary. I am not saying that we are constantly doing the wrong thing. But I am saying that if we didn't come up with a few wrong things before we figured out what was the best course of action, then we have probably made a much more uninformed decision than is good for us. Oh, and when you are wrong, say it. Say it out loud. Especially if you are in charge or leading. That is the number one way to get people to answer all of these questions with more veracity—show the value they had. I worked for a CEO once (who you will learn more about later) who regularly would get engaged in a conversation with his staff, at all levels, and when confronted with the realization that he was wrong would stop, take a breath, and say, "You know what, I do believe I was completely wrong on this. Thank you so much!" and then he would move forward in a different way with his new knowledge. He was still the CEO, he was still in charge, and he was more respected than ever. In fact, no one really doubted his decisions because anyone could second-guess them and, as a result, the final ones he made were considered to have weathered enough real challenge to be rock solid.

5. Am I okay with not knowing?

This is the **courage-to-be-humble question** that moves us forward even in the midst of ambiguity. It is the question for an agile mindset. I have spoken to leaders many times about the value of a team that will commit to things they don't know how to achieve. Well, we need to learn what we don't know, and understand that this will have to happen as we move forward. Leading with Learning Before Knowing is a matter of having the confidence, as well as the practices or behaviors (like the ones in this book), to move forward without knowing and to learn as we go. Whenever I think of this question, I see in my mind that scene from the film *Ghostbusters* when Bill Murray's character is being asked how they will do all these things that have never been done before and he gets this big smile, swigs from a bottle of whiskey, and says enthusiastically, "I don't know! I don't know!" It's just one more reason to want to be Bill Murray, but it is also the exact approach you need to take. "I don't know... but I will learn, so let's get going!" This is how we activate our heart of transformation.

Learning from the best—the art of self-interrogation

Interrogation. It is not a word that probably conjures up immediate warm and fuzzy thoughts. It sounds ominous and threatening. But the actual denotation of interrogation is simply to question closely, formally, and systematically. And since we should have our best interests at heart, who better to interrogate us than ourselves?

At the beginning of this chapter, I referenced my friend Bob Moesta, innovation guru extraordinaire, who has referred to his approach to innovation (a practice known as Jobs-to-be-Done Theory) as "interrogate to innovate," because of how he and his team approach their work. They will connect with a consumer of a product or service and have in-depth conversations with that person that get to the heart of the struggle that consumer is trying to overcome. There are some interesting lessons in what they do.

First of all, they access their ignorance. They don't pretend to know anything. In fact, they assume and state that they don't. They encourage the person they are interviewing to "Give it to me like you're making a documentary, tell me what happened, step by step—who did you talk to, what did you think, what did you say, what did they say, what happened then?—play the film for me in your mind and describe it. Assume that I don't know anything." The beauty of this approach is that it sidesteps the assumption trap. They don't assume anything, they ask about everything, and they start from a place of forced ignorance even if they have had prior experience. They want it to be fresh and free from their past assumptions so that they don't start looking for data to confirm what they already know (or think they know).

Second, and why they call it interrogation, is that their questions are seemingly without agenda. They are not trying to get any admission of something they already have hypothesized to be true. Instead, they are building connection. The best negotiators find a way to create a connection. Bob and team are friendly, folksy even, as they listen and probe and express real interest in what they don't know, not in proving what they think they know. This gets people to be much more introspective, to feel freer to explore and to actually not have to know everything themselves. They have de-escalated the need to know. It holds no value in the conversation and now they can move away into the unknown and just explore and discover. In fact, watching Bob and his partner-in-crime Greg Engle challenge each other on the assumptions they have made that still snuck in is one of the highlights of working with them. It is also a study in the power of humility.

Finally, they frame their thinking around one fundamental precept. The consumer they are talking to is looking for something to help them overcome what they are struggling with; to make progress. And it is the struggling moment that Bob says is at the heart of all innovation. The solution may be the thing that eventually makes you millions, but it has no meaning or value unless you have identified the problem it solves; the job it does. So, the work that Bob and The Re-Wired Group do is about problem finding. Once that work is done, the solving becomes the much easier part of the equation for innovation and success.

We are going to borrow from Bob for this next "making it real," which is about the art of the debrief.

Making it real—learning out loud; the art of the debrief

In Chapter 4 we discussed the value of asking our key questions three times, with your whole heart. We will now build on that with the second way of making it real—the art of the debrief. Debriefing ourselves (as well as others, of course) is where we actually learn. I believe it is critical to engage in Learning Out Loud. To me, that means we have to have a conversation with ourselves that is both systematic and formal as well as spoken out loud. So, yes, I am encouraging you to talk to yourself again. Below is your script for debriefing yourself and capturing what you are learning. When you use it the first few times, find a place where you can be alone and talk to yourself out loud. If this is challenging or just too weird for you at first, then find a friend or family member you trust, and have them ask you the questions in the script and then answer them out loud. Let them make notes for you and read back to you what they heard. Make sure you expressed it the way you meant to do. If not, try again until you get it right.

If you learn to debrief yourself, out loud, you will find that the amount of actual change you make will be markedly higher. There is plenty of research to support this but you don't even need to know that. Just do it, you'll see. (And, just to be clear, all of the making it real concepts and tools for transformation work with all of the questions for the six capabilities in this book, I am just giving them to you one at a time. When you are done you will have a full set of questions, for all of the capabilities, and a full set of ideas and techniques to truly make them real in your life and to help you transform. That's the goal.)

Tools for transformation—the debrief

So, you have used one or more of the Learning Before Knowing questions above. Here's how I want you to debrief it.

The six levels of debriefing

There are six levels of debrief that we are going to dive into. And I would be remiss not to say that some of the debrief questions you will see here I originally learned working with Michael Bungay Stanier. While he didn't invent the debrief, he improved greatly upon its use in helping us understand ourselves and each other in a simple and useful manner.

LEVEL 1—NOTICING WHAT HAPPENED

In this level of debrief we just want to pause, take a breath, and step back to observe ourselves. Graham Leicester calls this act of looking at what you are doing while you are doing it the genesis of psychological literacy.[7] It is a critical skill to develop in developing yourself. Here are our key questions:

- What was most useful?
- What was most interesting?

These questions are the juicy palate-cleansers of self-awareness. If you just start with deploying these two alone early on, that is okay. They have power unto themselves and will move you forward in becoming more insightful about what matters to you and what you believe to be true.

LEVEL 2—RECOGNIZE WHAT HAPPENED

Here is where we go a little deeper and start to make meaning out of what we see in ourselves. Making meaning is where we really begin to learn. It is how we determine what has value and where we might want to focus our efforts in developing our self-awareness. The key questions:

- What was the moment of recognition?
- What was the "ah-ha!" moment?
- What did you see that made you say, "I get it"?

Play back what was happening. What washed over you when you had that mental moment of your eyes opening? How did you feel about that? Did it feel like victory? Like growth? Was it like a new horizon was opening up? Hopefully it felt liberating and you began to think that there was more to things than what you knew.

LEVEL 3—SEE YOUR LIMITATIONS

These are the questions that push us to learn more. When we climb up a rung on the ladder of self-awareness, we are starting our journey anew. We have climbed over the top and found we are at the bottom of the next level to be climbed. That is amazing! Don't let it become dispiriting. No, we never reach the finish line but that just means that there are no limits to our growth. Here are the questions:

- What do I know now (that I didn't know before)?
- What am I starting to see that was unclear to me before?
- What do I need to know more about?

These questions will guide you as you journey up the mountain, they will help you pick the fork in the path that is best for you. Remember, this is not about just any journey, it is about *your* journey.

LEVEL 4—LOOK FOR HELP

No wise person undertakes a new adventure without preparation and without guidance. While asking for help has somehow become something that we are very poor at, it is critical for our growth. As discussed before, the world is just too complex and moving too fast for us to be lone superheroes. Ask for help, surround yourself with people who want to help you. Move faster together. The questions to ask are:

- Who can help me?
- Who knows about this?
- What would they do (and am I sure about that)?

LEVEL 5—MAKE A CHOICE

You have looked at what is going on, you've looked inside, and you've looked outside for help. Now it is time to put it into action. In order to make it real you have to make a choice. There are a lot of things you could probably do, and the vast majority should move you forward. None is the full answer, that is not to be expected, but they are a part of the answer and they are forward motion. So, you really have complete freedom to choose your first/next step. You can base it on which one just feels right, or which one seems easiest or that is most likely to succeed. It's up to you. But if you want additional guidance, here it is—pick the one you will follow through on and do. Picking one you will actually do is much better than any other choice you have. Here is the question, there is only one:

- What will I do first?

LEVEL 6—LOOK INSIDE YOURSELF

This level is actually one of the big leaps in making it real. The five before got us into action so that we are putting what we think we have learned to the test. And hopefully you are doing it three times with your whole heart. For this next level, where deeper learning can occur, you will need to both practice this and, at times, do it with someone you trust. Find someone who is willing to help you without giving you advice. Find that person who will let you learn out loud with them without imposing an agenda. Just find someone who loves you and cares about you. Oh, and it is unlikely that everything will become clear immediately. But once you answer the question(s) below, consider your answer a working hypothesis about how you operate. Find ways to test that hypothesis. Ask others if they see it or if it resonates with how they see you. I have often found that when I uncover a pattern about me that I had never seen before and then take it cautiously to people who know me well that they just smile, and I realize that they have been seeing it for years. I was the only one it was hidden from. So, here you go, the Level 6 questions of debriefing:

- What's the pattern?
- What habit have I not noticed before?
- What does this say about me?

These questions, especially the last, will help you look at what your own personal values are. They will help you uncover the power of your own ego and the role it plays in directing your behavior, unfettered if you let it. Finally, it helps you start to see the white lies you tell yourself in order to avoid shame and the fear of not being adequate, of being an imposter in the successes of your life. When you begin to see through your own lies you begin to see clearly the need to not cling so closely to what you know—to your truths—and to become a person of learning. Not a learned person, a learning person—and it takes a learning brain to pump a heart of transformation.

Endnotes

1 Agile (2019) Manifesto for Agile Software Development, *Agile* [online] http://agilemanifesto.org/ (archived at https://perma.cc/3PTR-D3LF)

2 Hess, E D and Ludwig, K (2017) *Humility is the New Smart: Rethinking human excellence in the smart machine age*, Berrett-Koehler, Oakland CA

3 Colvin, G (2016) *Humans are Underrated*, Nicholas Brealey, London

4 MacLean, P D (1990) *The Triune Brain in Evolution: Role in paleocerebral functions*, Plenum Press, London and New York

5 Curious for more info about the reptilian brain? Check out *Tame the Primitive Brain* by my dear friend Mark Bowden, a great and useful read. Bowden,

M (2013) *Tame the Primitive Brain: 28 ways in 28 days to manage the most impulsive behaviors at work*, John Wiley & Sons, New Jersey

6 Wallace, D F and College, K (2009) *This is Water*, Little, Brown, New York

7 O'Hara, M and Leicester, G (2019) *Dancing at the Edge: Competence, culture and organization in the 21st century*, Triarchy Press, Axminster

06

Changing Before Protecting

An intersection of friends

It's funny how parts of our own worlds collide and intersect. Michael Bungay Stanier is a thought leader in coaching and curiosity and how these both drive business success. He and I have been friends for over 15 years. We have traveled the world together, grown together, challenged each other, and had some truly wonderful nights out and some of the more memorable meals of my life. I first met Michael when he lived in Boston and I lived just outside New York before he became a bestselling author of books like *The Coaching Habit* and *The Advice Trap*. He is a close friend and a clear influence on who I have become, as you will have noted. But we will come back to Michael. Let me tell you another story.

Joe Whittinghill and I grew up together, but we didn't know that until we started talking during a hike in the California redwoods early on in the tenure of our cohort at Pepperdine University's renowned MSOD (Master of Science in Organization Development) program. It was one of those team-building, trust-fall kind of things to start developing the deeper relationships in the cohort we would need to survive and succeed in the demanding program. We were walking down the trail and he looked at me sort of quizzically, and maybe with some slight irritation in his voice, and asked me, "Where did you get that hat?"

The chapeau in question was a baby blue, and somewhat battered, corduroy cap from the Rocking R Bar in Bozeman, Montana. Being a boy from Montana and being quizzed about where I had got a hat from a legendary (at least to locals) Montana drinking institution was a bit surprising. And annoying, maybe, coming from some "preppie" consultant from Seattle, of all places, who I didn't know. He almost sounded proprietary, like I was wearing the hat illegitimately, as if I was some sort of poser who bought obscure bar hats to look cool (at least that is what my brain leapt to as one of many baseless assumptions). So, my slightly sardonic reply, "I got it at the Rocking R Bar," with no further explanation, might be understandable, if not so tolerant.

"Why were you at the Rocking R Bar?"

I'm a little more annoyed now.

"Because I'm from Montana."

"Where in Montana?"

I'm wondering what this inquisition is all about now.

"Billings."

"Which high school did you attend?"

I'm starting to get curious now.

"West."

"Central."

Looking at Joe now, and letting his surname register in my brain, I'm having a moment of clarity begin to dawn and it was my turn to ask a question.

"What did your dad do?"

With a smile slowly spreading across his face, Joe said, "My father was a pediatrician."

"Your father was my pediatrician my entire childhood."

To the best of our memories, Joe and I had never met before 1995, but it seems likely we must have anyway. We had many friends in common and Billings is not a sprawling metropolis by any means. But we became friends that day and our friendship continues to this day, despite being a continent apart and not seeing each other or talking to each other with great frequency.

Joe is Corporate Vice President of Talent, Learning, and Insights for Microsoft. He is a talented man and a good person who I am proud to have as a friend. When I was starting to tackle the capability of Changing Before Protecting, I immediately thought of Joe and his role in, and insight into, one of the greatest change stories of modern business—what Satya Nadella has done to rekindle Microsoft and bring about a second coming of the company that is perhaps even more successful than its legendary first coming. So, when I reached out, he responded immediately and squeezed me in for a very early morning call within a matter of a couple of days. We covered a lot of ground, but what we kept coming back to was a story that, in fact, I already knew from my conversations with Michael Bungay Stanier. But seeing it again, through a very different set of eyes, it became clear to me that this was the example I wanted to share as it captures what it means to not act like a leader, but to be a leader.

A story of not protecting

Jean-Philippe Courtois is Executive Vice President, and President of Sales, Marketing, and Operations at Microsoft. By anyone's standards he is an incredibly accomplished man with much to be admired. I do not know J P (as he is also referred to) personally and we have never met. But I know of him. At a company the size of Microsoft, he holds responsibilities bigger than those of most of the CEOs in the world and has a reputation and standing around the globe that is truly extraordinary. He led the group that drove Microsoft's growth to legendary levels, year after year. But, despite his immense business success, he does not stop there. Through his Live for Good Foundation, created in memory of his son, he provides a platform for, as their mission states, "Unlocking the potential of young people with diverse backgrounds through social entrepreneurship and accelerating positive innovation at the heart of an engaged community." They provide support and guidance to these young people to help them realize their dreams to change the world for better, for everyone.

J P is, by many accounts, a reserved and modest man. Not someone prone to boisterousness. A private man with a deep passion to make the world a better place. He is a critical partner-in-arms with Satya Nadella in realizing Microsoft's vision to empower everyone and every organization on the planet to achieve more. While his work would speak of a man who is deeply feeling, he is not known to be a man who is the proverbial "open book" of emotions, but someone who keeps his own counsel. In 2019, J P was on a stage at the Microsoft Ready conference, where they were launching work that Joe's team had tirelessly led. Work that helped them define what mattered at Microsoft—how to lead with purpose. As Joe stated in a recent article, their goal was, "clarifying the role of the manager and setting clearer expectations. Through our management excellence framework to **Model, Coach,** and **Care,** we not only ask managers to demonstrate a growth mindset, but also to help employees to define and understand their purpose and find ways to live that purpose at Microsoft."[1]

This brings me back to my friend Michael Bungay Stanier. As one part of Microsoft's efforts to support their managers with this framework, they have implemented programs across the company from Box of Crayons and Michael's book *The Coaching Habit.* They wanted their people to be "Learn-it-alls, not Know-it-alls," and the coach-like, curiosity-driven approach from Box of Crayons was one of the ways they were going to address that. They had done numerous live sessions for people across the company over the ensuing year as well as having launched a bespoke virtual program for the entire organization. But there is one truth we all really know about how we learn and embrace new ways and that is that we don't take our cues from what our leaders say but what they do. It was not enough to provide tools and training. What leadership was asking for from their people needed to be modeled. As a result, J P found himself sitting in front of thousands of Microsoft leaders being coached by Michael.

True coaching is not about giving advice, it is about asking questions. As Mary Beth O'Neill, a seminal figure in the field of executive coaching, says, it is about backbone and heart. Backbone meaning you will have the courage to speak the truth and help your client confront what really matters. Heart means that you will truly care about your client's needs and challenges and not let any potential uncomfortableness from you speaking the truth stand in your way of reaching out, engaging, and being there for your client.[2]

Coaching, done right, is not a comfortable process for anyone. It requires us to dig deeper into what is really at the core of our challenges and to face things that we have been working diligently to avoid facing, maybe for years. It requires us to disclose things that we find hard to disclose. It requires a willingness to be vulnerable, to be wrong, to learn, and to admit we need to change and grow. Having been on both sides of the coaching arrangement more times than I can count, I can tell you that it is uncomfortable and awkward and that, as the person being coached, you will feel exposed. But that discomfort is usually just experienced in front of the coach you have come to trust and with no one else present. Being coached by someone you don't really know, in front of thousands of people who respect and look up to you, when you are a person of acknowledged status and reserve, is a rare sight, and a deucedly uncomfortable place to be, I can only imagine. I once had someone tell me that I "have self-disclosure down to an art form." I think it was both a compliment and a minor insult. But, nonetheless, I have been coached live in front of smaller audiences a number of times through my work with Michael. It was a bit terrifying each time.

As I said, I don't know Jean-Philippe Courtois, but I admire him as a man of courage to do what he did. He chose not only to embrace Changing Before Protecting, but he did it out loud and on a stage in front of thousands of his colleagues. He chose to model change himself, not leave it to others. He sent a clear message; this is for all of us to learn and do. He showed his, and Microsoft's, commitment to Model, Coach, and Care.

Very early on in the live coaching, Michael asked a question to which J P, like most of us would, gave a somewhat safe and maybe surface answer. Michael's response was to pause and then say, "No, let's try this again," and repeat the question, lovingly but pointedly. This caused the entire room to erupt in laughter at the breaking of the tension of seeing this honest and naturally somewhat evasive response called out. It was culturally uncomfortable to see a highly respected leader going against type and putting himself in a difficult place just to show that doing this was valuable, if not easy. Michael re-asked the question with backbone and stayed with J P with heart. J P modeled changing by dropping his protection, and cared for the people he led by going deeper into things that really mattered—things that were not easy to say, or see in himself, and he let his own learning unfold. He led, and learned, out loud.

You may be wondering if I am going to relate the content of the coaching conversation here. I am not. In fact, I have avoided asking more about it, as I was not there, because what he explored was not public. Yes, I know, it was in front of thousands of people, but that was for the purpose of modeling change, not voyeurism, and the room had been asked to create a safe space by agreeing to keep the content of the dialogue confidential. Granted, it was an incredibly large safe space, but safe enough, nonetheless. That safety will be honored here. What I can say is that people left that room impacted by the courage and vulnerability J P showed and by the power of the simple coaching conversation that was role modeled. If an organization wants to embrace Changing Before Protecting, it takes the kind of out-loud leadership exemplified by leaders like Jean-Philippe Courtois.

It would have been easier, maybe, to talk about other aspects of Changing Before Protecting that have been a part of Microsoft's rekindling and reinvention. Their willingness to take the risk to sacrifice the financial juggernaut of Office in the box, to move to far less predictable cloud models, is a made for the Harvard Business Review (HBR) case study of overcoming *The Innovator's Dilemma*[3] and embracing change while at the top of your game. But, for me, these larger and more systemic examples of Changing Before Protecting are only made possible by the acts of individuals in embracing Changing Before Protecting for themselves. As stated earlier, organizations don't exist, only the people in them do. And people change one by one, not as an entity or a collective. Microsoft has not reinvented itself because of strategic decisions about product. They have done it person by person, leader by leader. The hard way. The only way.

But, let's use these Microsoft examples to explore the organization versus individual dichotomy a little deeper. And let's talk more about *protecting*. Why it mattered, why it still matters, but why it is no longer enough without being enfolded and transcended by *changing*.

Why protecting might not be good protection

Protecting. It sounds like a good thing. A great thing even. We protect our families, our friends, ourselves. Of course, we can be overprotective and not give people the opportunities they need to risk, fail, fall, and grow, as a result. Unwittingly depriving them of the opportunity to build the resilience they will need to walk through this world. But, all in all, protection is usually seen as more positive than negative.

When it comes to business, protection has been a very successful strategy for companies for years, and I am not advocating eliminating all the protections a company needs. Companies should protect themselves from brand or product infringement, working with less than ethical customers or partners, protecting intellectual property, and libelous and slanderous claims that can negatively impact a brand built through hard work and long effort. Where protection first starts to maybe get a bit ugly is in the form of protectionism where companies leverage (or influence the creation of) laws and policies that give them an unfair advantage over competition. While some will disagree, I think it shows up in the contractual obligations around "poaching" employees. If they want to go elsewhere then they are probably not the right person to remain or the company is no longer right for them.

But when we are talking here about protecting in comparison to changing, we are really talking about people, not policy. Particularly we are talking about ourselves and those we work closely with. As you read through this book, and think about the capabilities I am advocating, it will be easy to see these as reflecting organizational capabilities, which they are, but not in the way that might seem most obvious. When we talk about an organization's capabilities, we most often have in mind something that treats the organization as if it were an actual entity on its own, not the people who make it up. Let's take the example of this in what Microsoft did with Office.

Arguably, one of Steve Ballmer's smartest contributions to Microsoft's success was moving contracts from one-year to three-year terms. Why make the renewal sales efforts annually and deal with the unpredictability in revenue every year when you could save money and effort, and add certainty, by doing it every three years? For quite a while, that is how Office was sold. It was positioned as something you bought once, every three years. At the time, how much you used it and what value you actually got from it were not really looked at. When it came time to renew, companies looked at cost of operations, cost of competitive products, functionality, and cost of moving to a new system as key inputs for making a renewal decision. This proved to favor Office for companies that already had it in place and Microsoft developed a powerhouse of revenue and margin.

But when the move to the cloud happened, all that changed. Now, Microsoft had something that companies could engage and disengage in much more quickly. Value had to be shown on an almost daily basis, not just every three years, and in comparison to other products that would incur costly migration expense. But what is really interesting here is that Microsoft chose to do this. Why would they do that? They were on a really good run of protecting their business, it was a critical aspect of the move from one-year to three-year enterprise contracts. But they knew that protection was a point-in-time strategy. This is a critical lesson that most organizations never really learn, at least until it is too late. In a world where value was measured (and really only could be measured) at an enterprise-wide cost level, to protect that revenue made sense. But in the emerging world where deployment became simpler and web-based with minimal installation on local machines, as opposed to massive server-based enterprise installations, barriers to change were shattered. And in a world of big data, usage and value were much easier to calculate.

When Microsoft decided to make cloud a priority, it was not their strength (when was the last time you used Bing to search the internet instead of Google?). But the writing in the sky was fairly clear. Still, it was painful to risk the protected revenue they had for the open market of cloud-based software as a service (SaaS) products. Nonetheless, they saw that the time for protecting was over and they needed to get ahead of it, despite the cost, if they were to lead what was coming next. It was a bold move that has paid off significant dividends. Along the way, Microsoft has refocused its relationship with customers from one of negotiation to one of partnering. Helping customers understand how Office is being used, what aspects of it are being used the most, what is being underused, how they can extract more value from what is available, and, probably most importantly to many customers, basing cost on value realized. This is a far less one-sided arrangement. But it also is developing a far more trusting partnership with customers and opens up a whole world of customers of all sizes. Remember Microsoft's mission under Satya Nadella's leadership? "Empower everyone and every organization on the planet to achieve more"? It was this mission that drove the change, and the change that helped move them closer to achieving the vision.

This is a great example of an organizational capability of Changing Before Protecting. But it is easy to mistake this organizational capability as something that is simply in the water at Microsoft. It is not. In fact, this was a change that did not happen easily, there was blood, sweat, and tears. It took a committed leader, Satya Nadella, working one-on-one with individuals on his team. Some took his vision for their own, some didn't and, as a result, left. Then it took individuals looking at all the systems in place that supported the old ways and dismantling and rebuilding them one by one. Rewards systems, hiring systems, training systems, management processes, sales capabilities, organizational structure, the list goes on and on. And each of these areas needed individuals who understood, aligned, and worked through the changes needed and then championed those changes in the face of opposition, lack of understanding, and fear. So, yes, Changing Before Protecting is becoming an organizational capability at Microsoft but it is being accomplished person by person. That is why when we decide we need to shift our capabilities to the ones at the heart of transformation, we do it by individual behaviors and acts starting in the form of asking new questions.

So, how do individuals change?

The five questions of Changing Before Protecting

Change. It's a big game but played by one player at a time. Let's talk about how to play that game. The question now becomes, "What questions help us to step away from the faux safety of Protecting into the place of uncertainty and growth that is Changing?" Here they are.

Question 1: What's the worst that could happen?
Question 2: What's the cost of staying safe?
Question 3: What am I afraid to do?
Question 4: How can I lead out loud here?
Question 5: When did I last ask for help?

---

1. What's the worst that could happen?

This is the **question that puts a name on our fears.** Remember that our brain craves certainty. Changing places us squarely in the path of uncertainty. But we are (hopefully) a little more evolved and living in a slightly different world from the one where most choices literally were life and death. But our instinctual brain doesn't split these fine hairs. Uncertainty appears as a nondescript black hole of doom to the unconscious mind, so you need to take a deep breath and put the neocortex to work. As Mama used to say, "Use your words!" So, pause and take a few deep breaths to let some oxygen-rich blood fill your brain and then ask the question, "What's the worst that could happen?" And you can take your time with this one. Sometimes I white board it out and even add odds to the mix. I don't know how bad the worst will be for you or how likely it is, but I am willing to wager that it is far more often than not much less dangerous and much less likely than you imagine at first. The most common answer I get when coaching people with this question is, "Well, I'll find out that it (whatever it is) won't work!" When we discuss this, the next realization is that they have just assumed it won't work, but they really don't know. So, the worst thing that is happening is that they are actually confirming something they have already assumed to be true, and acting as if it were true, without ever challenging it. But they will never know if they were wrong and they will always remain stuck if they don't find out. It is a very curious phenomenon to think, "It might not go my way, so I better just assume it won't and move on." But this is often what happens. Sound familiar?

2. What's the cost of staying safe?

This is the **reality-check question**. I love having this discussion because the question itself challenges the idea that safe is better. We discussed the downside of protecting above, but we still crave safety and usually mistake that craving for a virtue. But what advances have been made, what greatness accomplished, what victory has ever been achieved, by playing it safe? Now I'm not recommending foolish recklessness, but in our quest to avoid danger we forget to examine the danger of playing it safe. So, make a list. What opportunities will be sacrificed? What advances cannot be made? What prizes cannot be won? I can't tell you with certainty what it takes to be great, but I can tell you that those who have never taken the risks to be great, never will be.

3. What am I afraid to do?

This is the **find-your-fear question**. If the first two questions helped us minimize the size of "worst" and question the virtue of "safe," this question helps us place our selves squarely in the middle of the equation of changing and protecting. You could almost say that this question is a combination of the first two, personalized and internalized. "What is the worst that could happen *to me*?" "What is the cost of staying safe *for me*?" These are hard questions to ask and harder to answer. Fear is a monster. I believe that nearly all human actions can be explained by fear, shame, and the desperate desire to avoid both. I know that sounds kind of negative, but I don't think it has to be. Fear, in particular, is a guide. It is often a guide to where we need to go, as strange as that may sound. What we fear is telling us what we value. Am I afraid to call out my colleague on the racist thing he said? I probably want equality and justice for all but know the fight might cost me. Am I afraid to get up on that stage? I probably have something to say that I believe matters, but I realize that I would have to live up to my own rhetoric. Do I fear the unknown? Then I probably am dissatisfied with the current situation and strongly desire change, but I cannot be guaranteed to get it. I can, however, be guaranteed to have what I already have. At least for now. When you ask yourself what you are afraid to do, you begin to look at the core of who you are and, when you finally admit to your dreams and hopes, it hurts even more not to go after them. But what is the cost of never finding your true purpose in the first place? Well, among other things, you will miss making the most of the one life you were given. There are no do-overs.

4. How can I lead out loud here?

This is the **power-of-vulnerability question**. "Lead out loud." It is probably not a phrase I invented. But it is one that I use often and in a specific way. For me, leading out loud is to have asked the questions above, the ones that take you to a course of action, and then putting it "on a stage." In the example of Jean-Philippe Courtois, he was literally on a stage in front of several thousand people. But for some of us the stage is a small meeting or even just sitting with one other person. The key aspect of it is that it is in front of at least one other person— that you are modeling how you are changing for the benefit of others. This can come at the cost of awkwardness, misunderstanding, and fumbling through something for the first time. But people learn by what they see is happening, not what they are told to do. Listen and learn? It's a myth. Watch and learn? That is the reality. So, once you have figured out that the worst is not so dire, once you have realized that the cost of staying safe is high, once you know where fear is telling you to go, then do what you are going to do in front of others so they can find inspiration and take comfort in not being so alone when they do the same. In organizations, you enhance their feeling of psychological safety to do the same, if you are a leader. So, if you are a leader, lead out loud. Otherwise you might be just a manager.

5. When did I last ask for help?

This is the **litmus-test question** that tells you how much you are actually embracing your own change. We simply cannot see ourselves through the eyes of others. We make up our own internal narrative (often to make us feel better) but we have no way of knowing if the changes we are making are seen by others and having an impact on the world around us. One of the best ways not only to change, but find out if we are actually changing, is not to try to change on our own. First of all, asking this question challenges others to change. Second, it helps us see needs and opportunities we might have missed. Third, we begin to get feedback on whether we are really taking on a meaningful or a mediocre change. People get excited to help with real change; they get much less excited with cosmetic ones. Change is a team sport executed by a mix of individuals. The network changes when the nodes change. Engage other nodes in your change and they will engage you in theirs and things will start to happen.

Learning from the best—the virtue of small recoverable tests

So, now it's time to make some changes. You have asked yourself the questions in this chapter and they have led you to some conclusions. You have realized that the worst may not be the worst, that staying put is not actually staying safe, that your fear can guide you, that you need to change on stage, and that help is a good thing.

But what if the changes you are about to attempt are not actually the best thing to do? Are you sure you want to make these changes? Now, hold on, don't toss this book out in frustration. I know I have been championing change hard. However, protecting yourself is not bad in and of itself, it's just not enough anymore. Protecting can be a great strategy, if changing is not. As mentioned above in the Microsoft example, protecting is a point-in-time strategy. The problem is that many people continue to assume they are at that point in time and remain in protecting mode for too long. That is why we start with changing, to discover if this is the time for protecting.

The wrinkle is that you cannot always know. The insidious aspect of Changing Before Protecting is that you don't know the impact of changing until you make the change. Let's reflect back on the first question above—what's the worst that could happen? Sometimes, the worst is actually fairly bad. Some changes are small risks, some are large. Do we then only take the small risks? No, that is not the answer. The answer is that, when you can, you may take smaller risks that help you test the value of the change you want to make.

I first learned about this approach from Bob Kegan and Lisa Lahey. It is a key part of their Immunity to Change framework cited earlier. In their theory, once you have an assumption that you want to challenge, you do it by testing out aspects of it that, if your theory is wrong, don't devastate you. Their guidance is sound. If the worst is actually potentially fairly bad, then what can you do to help you learn and test without crossing the point of no return? Here is an example.

In the early 1990s I was studying for my MBA at Pepperdine University in southern California. I had left college with an undergraduate degree in psychology and no idea what to do with it. Initially my plan was to be a clinical psychologist, and I was excited about this plan right up until the point that I wasn't. In my senior year, I began to doubt that this was what I wanted to do. Somehow it had lost its luster, I really don't even recall why. Maybe, after doing some internships and practicum in psychotherapy, I started to realize that I had very little control over who I would be counseling and what we would focus on. But I didn't know what else to do. I had applied to one graduate school program only. It was a PhD program with an outstanding university that also provided full-ride scholarships to the selected students. That year they received over 400 qualified applications. They only chose eight. I made it to the last 16 and then was placed on the alternate list, but no one declined their offer, so I was not accepted. Somehow, in my 22-year-old brain I thought this was an indication that this was not my path.

However, I still needed a job and needed to figure out how to grow up and pay my own way. A good friend of mine had started working for the Social Services Agency in Orange County, California, the one that (somewhat famously) went bankrupt in 1994.[4] She told me that just having a college degree and being willing to work there was usually enough to get hired and so, not really knowing what options I had, I applied and got the job as an Eligibility Worker (yes, that was actually the inspiring job title) for OCSSA. I was now the welfare man, assessing applicants' eligibility for various aid programs.

I could write another book on that experience, but it would not be a fun read. My experience was far from positive. With so many regulations and interests involved it did not appear that the organization was designed as much as assembled from disparate parts. I experienced things that I would tell my clients now are inefficient and disengaging, at the very least. I would not want a similar job again, for many reasons. But something interesting came out of that work experience; I got really curious as to how an organization could be run the way it was.

All around me were obvious fixes to clear problems, but any mention of these was met with the mild derision of telling me that I was young and thought I knew it all and I just needed to sit back and learn. I think they meant learn to accept "the way it is" and not worry about it. It couldn't be changed so just do your job, keep your head down, earn your money and take care of yourself. I've been wrong many times in my career, there is no doubt about that. But, looking back at that experience I can tell you honestly that this was not one of those times and, fortunately, history bears out that this was not the most well-run organization at that time. But I was able to do one thing that really felt good and really made me curious. Looking back now I'd say I engaged in a business process redesign but at the time I just said, "Why don't we do this?"

On the first of each month, homeless aid recipients would come into the office in person to collect their nominal cash aid and food stamps. At the time, the wait was on average six to seven hours to finally get processed and receive aid. There were several steps involved and each participant in the step had no visibility into what was happening in earlier steps or later steps and no one had any account-ability for the overall process for any one recipient. You just did your part and put some paper in a tray and grabbed the next paper out of another tray, that was it. But not all of these steps needed to rely on each other, some could be done independently and at the same time. But that wasn't the way it worked. After watching, and participating in, this disconnected process for a few cycles, I had some suggestions. My immediate manager, who was a nice woman and liked me, cautioned me about the dangers of having ideas "above my pay grade" and said that I needed not to come up with something that made me look smarter than those above her. She guided me into a smaller and more recoverable test of my theory about workflow. I could have taken my frustration, designed something that I thought was perfect, and brought it to leadership and said, "I've solved the problem that you've apparently been unable to, I hope you're smart enough to accept it!" And, believe me, I said it internally to myself probably 100 times! What she counseled me to do was to raise the issue as if it was one that had come from them and then to ask if I could take some time to look at possibilities to address the problem. Next, she had me present those ideas, with a couple of slightly differ-ent but equally useful approaches, and then ask them for their guidance. She also had me leave out one or two aspects of solutions that I already had and that were going to be fairly obvious to anyone listening to my pitch.

The result was that I approached the leadership with humility (of which I didn't have much, in regard to this, to be honest) and in the spirit of collaboration so that what was created was not seen as just mine. It was seen as my responding to a need they had identified, and I had come up with some ideas that they had then helped me refine. They now had ownership of the solution too. Interestingly, there had never really been any request of leadership to address the problem, but when I acted as if there had been no one disputed that, they just nodded and appreciated someone listening to what they hadn't actually said!

So, my small recoverable test was to pitch it as a response to their needs, not something I had identified without them, and see if they agreed. If they did not, which seemed highly unlikely, I could simply say that I must have misunderstood. This would not be a crime in their eyes, and they would see that I was ready to do more, but I had just not picked the right thing to go above and beyond on. The second was to pitch ideas as approaches that were not fully formed so that we could collaborate and they could build on the ideas, even if that was not needed by me. Instead of saying "This is **the** way," I could say, "I think this is a possible way, but how could you make it better?" If they thought I was wrong, I had not committed, I was just learning. And if they liked the idea, they could share ownership.

I took small and recoverable steps and tests to get to the point that I could obtain the buy-in to put the plan in action. Now, some of you may be thinking that I missed an opportunity to get the credit for my approach, which I did in part. I was still thanked and recognized for "my part" in the overall effort and was not the lone hero. But I was learning that playing a longer game can be much more useful than playing a shorter game. I got some credit for my work and they recognized me, among my peers, for the work I did. But they also recognized me for being a team player with potential and, maybe more importantly, not a threat to authority. Even more interesting is that I had stumbled into doing work process redesign without knowing it. And, in interviews for other roles later in my career, no one cared how it got done, they were interested in my ability to conceive of the idea and to sell it. I got the credit when and where it really mattered, just not as much the first time with the organization I was with. But it was much more valuable to have been able to successfully be a key part of something that happened as opposed to having a great idea that I never got to implement.

Your small recoverable tests will be different. The idea is to think of a first step, determine how you measure success, and make sure you learn from it. Put the debrief process to work. Don't get caught up in the immediate success only, focus on the learning. This will help you understand your best approach for making changes in your organization. The same goes for personal changes.

Let's say that I wanted to change my leadership approach, which I have multiple times over my career. When I was at Gartner, I ran a team of extraordinary professionals. Most of them had been chief information officers (CIOs) at major companies, many of them were older than me. It is not me being self-effacing to say that in any other company or situation I could easily have been working for many of them. Suffice it to say, it was a daunting situation, especially when the business grew to the point that I was appointing vice presidents to run teams and now I had a large, international team of leaders leading individual contributors who were highly experienced leaders in their own right.

My management style was very collaborative, open, and non-directive. People seemed to love that... most of the time. But there were definitely times when I sensed their frustration with the long conversations where so many opinions were shared, and we looked for consensus. I began to realize that, in some of these situations, I had to make a change. But I was afraid to do it. My working assumption was that I was able to lead this iconoclastic group through my inclusion and treating them as peers, not subordinates. I hate the word subordinates. Hierarchy is not my thing. Nonetheless, it has its value and there are many who are more comfortable in the clarity of the hierarchy.

When things would go wrong in these meetings it was usually when another voice or two emerged and began to really stand out from the group. Often, it was a voice of "no" not a voice of "yes." They were not offering collaborative solutions but were telling you why the ones being offered would not work. This was not, in my belief, done out of malice but done out of frustration and lack of leadership, in their view. They saw me as abdicating the role of taking the lead and just making the choice and they were not comfortable with that. They were worried we would just dither along, and it would impact us negatively. So, the naysaying would commence.

In consultation with someone in the group who also was someone I trusted to help me, I determined that this was a situation in which I needed to give people the comfort of decisive leadership. I was still apprehensive but a change was needed, that much had become clear, so I decided on a first step—to try it on once, but clearly, and then get feedback to see how it landed. In the next group session, we got into a discussion about our strategy for achieving the year's targets. One voice began to rise above in the naysaying, and I could see the body language begin to shift. So, I took a deep breath and spoke. "Okay, let me just pause you there. First, thank you for your views on this, you know I value your opinion. But we have to make a choice and, since we are not united in what to do, it falls to me. I have heard you and I disagree. So, unless anyone else has some information that hasn't been surfaced, we are going to proceed the way I've outlined and I expect your full and enthusiastic support of our direction. Do I have that?"

Honestly, the person looked a bit shocked, but then said, "Yes, if that's the decision you know I will support you."

Walking out of that meeting I felt like I had insulted that person, that I had not acted "like me," that people felt I was being foolish and bossy and acting like I knew better when I didn't. But I hadn't yet got feedback and I thought that, if what I was thinking was all true, I could apologize to that person and the team and go back to the way it was. But I didn't need to chase after feedback—it came running into my office all afternoon. It went something like this:

- "Thank you for taking control and shutting that down, you did the right thing."

- "You showed real leadership in there, we are all so opinionated that sometimes we just need to be told, 'enough already,' and be reminded that we have had our say but now we have to move forward."

- "We need more of that, and we all felt your presence and direction and we trust you."

It was wonderful, and truly surprising feedback, but the best was yet to come. It came from the person I had needed to shut down. "I just want you to know that I appreciate that you always listen, and I know I can get a bit strident about things. But I respect you as a colleague and a leader and I will be the first person to make sure that your direction is followed, and I will make it work. Thank you for being clear."

So, again, it was a test I could recover from. I knew success looked like me being seen as a leader, not a jerk, and that I needed to debrief it to learn and determine what to do next. I have incorporated that approach, when needed, into my leadership ever since. It has made me a better leader who continues to learn to lead in more effective ways as time goes on.

When bold changes are needed

Sometimes, small recoverable tests are not an option. Sometimes we have to choose and take the big risk of Changing Before Protecting. Sometimes we have to bet the farm, proverbially speaking. For some of us, it is when we leave a job that makes us unhappy, especially the ones that pay us really well and give us great status but that really cause us pain. At these times you need to gather the evidence, look at the data, and see that the unknown is scary but the known is killing your soul. These bold change moments usually come much less frequently than the smaller changes that we can test. But they do come and the follow-up is much the same as the small changes— know what success looks like and have a plan to learn. This is why I regularly get hired to help very senior leaders in new roles. They will include contracting with me as a part of their negotiation for the new role. They will be confident in their need for help in making the transition to a new top leadership role. While it feels uncomfortable at first, almost without fail the hiring companies see the wisdom in their investing in integrating their leadership approach to the company culture and being very thoughtful in how they develop their voice and style in the company to have the greatest impact the soonest.

Only you can decide when it is time for a bold change. They are the hardest to make and the easiest as well. They are hard because the risks are high. They are easy because they are big, and you cannot hide from them. There is no turning back from the bold change. Sometimes it is these bold changes that are the most transformative.

What I would advise you is to look back through those bold changes you have made in your life and look for the patterns that emerge. For me, one pattern is that I always live through it. And here's the thing, you will too! Therein lies the power of bold changes. Once you make one, you start to realize that change is possible, and that protection might be leading to stagnation. While you don't always have to jump off the cliff, sometimes you will find that summoning up the courage to do so puts you in a whole new place and the blood pumping furiously through your heart of transformation makes you stronger than you thought you were.

Endnotes

1   Whittinghill, J (2020) Purpose in a Digital Organization [online] https://www.hrps.org/resources/people-strategy-journal/fall2020/pages/feature-whittinghill.aspx (archived at https://perma.cc/U74N-YK22)
2   O'Neill, M B (2007) *Executive Coaching with Backbone and Heart: A systems approach to engaging leaders with their challenges*, Jossey-Bass, San Francisco
3   Christensen, C M (2016) *The Innovator's Dilemma: When new technologies cause great firms to fail*, Harvard Business Review Press, Boston MA
4   Orange County Register (2019) Here's How Orange County Went Broke 25 Years Ago [online] https://www.ocregister.com/2019/12/06/heres-how-orange-county-went-broke/ (archived at https://perma.cc/A7VZ-8MBF)

07

Pathfinding Before Path Following

A story of pathfinding

I am going to tell you a story of my own now, a story of pathfinding. We will discuss the truth that, while knowing clearly where you are going is absolutely necessary, just knowing and sharing the goal is not enough. How we will get there, the values that bind us together, are even more important. Destinations will change, and are changing faster than ever before, so how we journey matters more than it ever did.

In the mid-1990s, Abitibi-Price was the largest newsprint producer in the world. It traced its history back to 1820 when the William Price Company began exporting lumber to Great Britain from Canada. Canadian-based, but with a global footprint, Abitibi had grown in the 1990s under the leadership of CEO Ron Oberlander. What remains of Abitibi-Price, after many mergers, acquisitions, and (mostly) consolidations, is the company Resolute Forest Products of Montreal, Quebec. The global footprint for newsprint is, of course, greatly diminished in a world of digital media and Abitibi-Price is probably a name you do not know. But part of the story of what was once "the finest manufacturer and marketer of paper for communication" is one you need to hear.

To tell the story, I want to first tell you about Ron Oberlander. To do that, I am going to reprint for you here an excerpt from Ron's obituary from *The Globe and Mail* in Toronto after his passing from cancer on April 2, 2003. In it they talked about how skilled he was as a communicator and how he challenged people to do their best, speaking with an open mind at all times. They had this to say about his impact on the business:

> He convinced 14,000 people to believe in themselves and, in so doing, changed the course of a dying Canadian icon and paper industry giant. Under his leadership, Abitibi-Price became an organization where conversations for possibility replaced water cooler gossip, where meritocracy reined over hierarchy and where the collective energy of the whole produced the company's most substantial contributions in history for the benefit of its stakeholders. (*The Globe and Mail*, 2003)

They went on to talk about his legacy of developing young people and how those who became his students in business and life went on to leadership roles across Canada and, indeed, across the world. I was one of those students and I will be forever thankful for having encountered a senior leader like Ron Oberlander. The impact of who he was, and that experience, has grown influence over the years and inspired me to be the kind of leader that he was.

I was privileged to work under Ron's leadership when I was Vice President of Human Resources and Organization Development at the company's US-based sales and service corporation. Ron, being the person so lovingly and accurately described above, knew that he wanted to build a company that was "vision and values driven." And we wanted to do this in an incredibly volatile market with a company with a long and difficult, even dispirited, history. With the partnership of Jean-Claude Casavant, Executive Vice President of Organizational Leadership and Innovation (OLIN), he did just that. OLIN, by the way, was what most organizations call HR nowadays. Jean-Claude indeed had all the responsibilities of the Chief Human Resources Officer for the company. But both he and Ron were not interested in the somewhat cold sobriquet of "Human Resources" and preferred to lead with what mattered most to them—leadership and innovation.

One of the reasons for that is because life in the newsprint industry was not a run-of-the-mill experience (pun intended), it was a wild roller-coaster ride of dramatically fluctuating markets and unexpected disruptions. Without leadership and innovation, you could not survive. When I was first approached by Jean-Claude to consider joining Abitibi, we were classmates in Pepperdine University's Master of Science in Organization Development program (MSOD). I'll never forget the words of another classmate, who actually had experience with the pulp and paper industry, when he said, "Do you know anything about the newsprint industry? Oh man! It's a bloodbath of a market... it's a wild ride!" And indeed, it was. Using rough numbers, the company probably broke even if the price of newsprint was around US $450 per metric ton. In my first management team meeting the group was debating if the market was ready for them to take the price from a near record high of $780 a ton to $810, and there was great confidence this would be accepted by the market, bringing in amazing profits. Within less than a year we were discussing how to survive the current price of $380, which was still dropping and was at an unsustainable level of loss if we were to remain in business.

The newsprint market was driven by perception of supply and how that impacted demand. Demand could fluctuate by newspapers reducing the size of their sheets or the number of pages printed if the supply tightened and the prices grew too high. Once supply started to build up and demand dipped, one of the producers would eventually flinch and the price would drop. That small amount of actual tonnage became "ghost tonnage" in the market, seemingly everywhere and yet nowhere to be found, and everyone started cutting prices to be able to continue to produce and ship. It was a fascinating cat-and-mouse game between the producers, like Abitibi, and the publishers, as both sought to find a path that favored their competing interests. Overall profitability only worked out in aggregate, if it worked at all, and it was never smooth.

In a business with so much volatility, you had to have people who could think fast, react, strategize, and move quickly and locally, all while still coordinating globally. Strange to say, but this most decidedly old-school company really needed to be nimble like a tech startup, in many ways, to succeed. And success for newsprint companies was not easy to come by. When Ron Oberlander took over at

Abitibi-Price the company was languishing from years of poor management by its owners, once going completely into receivership, and was struggling to survive. It was also, in many of the small Canadian towns in which it operated, basically the sole economy of the town. Closing down a mill did not mean just a loss of jobs; in a very real way it meant the loss of an entire community and way of life.

So, what did Ron do? How did he lead Abitibi-Price to become "an organization where conversations for possibility replaced water cooler gossip, where meritocracy reined over hierarchy and where the collective energy of the whole produced the company's most substantial contributions in history for the benefit of its stakeholders"? He did it with vision and values.

I have worked with a lot of different companies over the years. To the best of my knowledge, all of them had a vision or mission statement and written values or cultural hallmarks that they touted as critical to their success. To be honest, I cannot recall for you what they were, in total or with any accuracy, for any of those companies… save one. At Abitibi-Price our vision was "To be the finest manufacturer and marketer of papers for communication." And our values were flexibility, continuous learning, moving with urgency (or velocity, as we also called it), business-like thinking and wise spending. I left Abitibi in 1999, but who we were as a company has never left me.

Ron and Jean-Claude had a very clear and simple approach; live the values to achieve the vision. Working under these two leaders was when I first saw the value of pathfinding over path following. It was not that we didn't have goals and targets, as a publicly traded company we most certainly did, but how we got there was, again, simple. We met, we discussed the options openly, and we made the choices that were congruent with who we said we were—that aligned with our values.

Of course, it was not an overnight journey to this place of openness and healthy conflict. Ron and J C instituted a rigorous effort to ensure that we acted like adults, told the truth (the whole truth), and built trust. Working with a small consulting organization (Roundstone International) we grew as people. Leslie Tucker and Juan Mobili from Roundstone helped us learn to put the background conversation in the foreground and to work together like fully functioning adults. With those capabilities, we decided together the day-to-day and year-to-year courses of action that aligned to who we said we were.

Let me give you a concrete example. At one point, our chief financial officer (CFO) brought forth the concern that our expenses were running "hot" and that we were likely to miss some important targets unless we could reduce overall expenses, mostly in sales and service, by 10 percent. Now, our sales teams traveled the globe and they met with publishers and owners of communications companies, many of whom were community and society leaders, political influencers, and very wealthy people. Entertainment was common and, given the commodity nature of the product, relationships were critical.

It was suggested by someone in the finance department that we undergo a rigorous cost evaluation exercise and then make a detailed plan of what could and could not be spent and then put in mechanisms to monitor and enforce this spending. They wanted to create a foolproof path to the cost reduction target of 10 percent (which was in the hundreds of millions), step by step and dollar by dollar. Then, at an executive team meeting, another senior leader realized that it was not path following that was needed, it was pathfinding. So, he spoke up. "No," he said, "we don't need to do that. Here is what we should do. Everyone, please ask your teams to cut their expenses down by at least 10 percent. They know what wise spending is and they are businesslike thinkers. They can figure out where best to cut their costs to reach the goal. For example, tell them when they have dinner with an important client to go to a nice place, but not the best, find that good place that is 10 percent less expensive. They can still order a decent bottle of wine, but order one that is at least 10 percent less than they might normally get. They all know what they spend, they understand flexibility and can find 10 percent in a way that allows them to do their jobs. And they can do it with urgency. That's it. If you say that, and if you also do that yourselves, we will find our way to reducing our current expenses."

Now, even in a company that had embraced letting people use the vision and values to find the path, that felt a bit out of control for the CFO. But he agreed. Three months later the expense run rate for the quarter was nearly 15 percent below the previous quarter and holding steady. There was no need for complicated policies and predetermined paths to achieve the outcome, paths that I have seen fail to reach the goal countless times elsewhere. No, there were simply the shared values of a culture that allowed people to find their own path to the goal.

You may wonder how else it was that this company you have probably never heard of came to understand and embrace its vision and values. Well, it wasn't because HR put up posters. I actually don't remember seeing any posters or placards about the values. But I do remember the values themselves because our leaders lived them. The values were the real power in the organization and the leaders followed them—and they demanded the same of others. Anyone in the company could call out Ron Oberlander if he was doing something they felt was not aligned with the values and he would stop, listen, and if they had a point he would concede, thank them, and immediately change course. But he also went further.

Once, at a big sales conference, Ron finished his opening remarks and then left the stage and, while sales leadership took over, he casually wandered down to the back of the room. He took an empty seat at a table occupied by some new salespeople he did not recognize. At a break in the proceedings, he turned to one and said, "Hi, I'm Ron." To which the salesman, whom we will call Bill, stammered back, "Er, yeah, I know, I saw you on stage. I'm Bill." "It's nice to meet you Bill. How long have you been with us?" "About three months." "Great. Can I ask you a question? Tell me, what do you think of our vision and values as a company?" "Well," Bill started out slowly but then picked up speed, "Yeah, I think they're great, just great!" Ron paused and then said, "Bill, do you know what our vision and values are, and can you tell me what they are, right now?" Bill's smile faded as he realized he had been caught lying to the CEO upon their first meeting. "No, no sir I can't," he said, crestfallen. "Bill, who do you work for, who is your manager?" "Luc." Ron looked up and spotted Luc and waved him over. Bill waited, ashen faced, to be reprimanded and, in his mind, probably fired. "Luc, this is Bill, he's been here about three months now." Luc chuckled, "Yeah, Ron, I know, I hired him." "Oh, well, Bill and I were talking, and he doesn't know what our vision and values are." "Yeah, sorry, I've been planning to talk with him about that, but we've just been so busy with customers since he arrived." "Oh," replied Ron, and then he paused a moment and then repeated, "Luc, this is Bill, he's been here about three months now and he doesn't know what our vision and values are." It was Luc's turn to pause, "He'll know them by heart and know what they mean by the end of the week and we will make it the focal point of our conversations from here on."

Ron smiled and then turned to Bill. "Bill, you're a good man. You not knowing the vision and values is not on you, that's on Luc, and he's clear now on what matters. You and I, Bill, we are good! Live our vision and values and you are going to have a long and successful career here and I could not be happier to have you working with me in this company that I love. Welcome to Abitibi!"

Ron was right about Bill, he was successful. And he didn't have to tell Bill what the steps of the path were, he simply gave him the destination and showed Bill how he walked the path himself; by living the values and leading out loud.

And Abitibi? Well, in 1997 they merged with Stone-Consolidated to form Abitibi-Consolidated, by far the biggest pulp and paper company in the world. In the course of the merger, they promised the Street synergy savings of US $100 million. Now if you know anything about mergers and acquisitions, the vast majority end up missing targets grievously and destroying shareholder value. They all have detailed plans and paths to achieve the declared goals of the merger, but fall short, nonetheless. Abitibi-Consolidated, as a merger of equals, with the added complication of being led by two co-CEOs for the first two years after the merger, more than doubled the savings goal to in excess of $200 million. We had a goal. We had values to guide us. We found a path.

While the changing realities of our digital world have reduced the newsprint industry into something much smaller and different, and while Ron has long since passed, the lessons I learned as a young leader there were the foundation of my career ever since. I've never worked anywhere like it again. But if I have one dream for this book and my contribution to the world it will be that other companies out there will move a little closer to being the kind of place I found when I had the great good fortune to work for men like Ron Oberlander and Jean-Claude Casavant. They showed me how to find the path by knowing what star to follow, what principles to make choices by, and how to stand for something as I found my way.

From following the path to finding the path

Tom Peters and Robert Waterman published *In Search of Excellence* back in 1982, based on research conducted in 1979–80. Even then, this wildly bestselling book emphasized the need to have clear vision and values to guide choices. It triumphed the value of the small group and the ability for people to innovate, be independent, and be entre-preneurial within a company. They highlighted that, while financial metrics, business process controls, and planning had value, they told only an impartial story without the ability of individuals to challenge and change their organization. *In Search of Excellence* became a kind of bible for corporations, a ubiquitous guidebook for being better. So, what happened? Why is it that so many organizations celebrated the new gospel of excellence in business but then quickly returned to their old command-and-control ways, if they ever really left them?

There have been interesting longitudinal studies done over time about the companies written about in *In Search of Excellence* show-ing their rising and falling fortunes. Another business classic is Jim Collins's book *From Good to Great* where he followed a number of companies over a long time to determine what made some last and what made some languish. Unfortunately, as time moved forward some of those great companies ceased to be great by his measures, calling into question some of the conclusions of the book. But I am not interested in going back to look at books like *In Search of Excellence* or *From Good to Great* to either laud or pillory them as tools of prognostication. What I think is interesting is that the ideas they proposed (like starting with "getting the right people on the bus") are ideas that, by and large, appear to be really good ones—ideas that can help drive the capabilities needed for our digital world today. No, what interests me is that we had so many good ideas and answers in front of us that we just didn't follow. Oh sure, we talked about them and we even championed them. But, in the end, most organizations did very little about them.

There are exceptions. In early 2014, Satya Nadella succeeded Steve Ballmer as CEO of Microsoft. Much has been written about what Satya has accomplished in the short years since he became CEO, not least what Satya himself shared in his book *Hit Refresh* where he talks at length about setting a "North Star" for the company and about focusing on building a culture that would be based on empathy, allowing for all to take more risks and listen to each other, and their customers, more closely and with the perspective of the other in mind.[1] In doing this, he has reinvented Microsoft's culture and the company has truly embarked on meaningful transformation. Not everything is perfect, not everyone is there yet, but the intent is clear, and the leaders are role modeling the very human (and empathetic) behaviors so many companies have spoken about, and sought to adopt, with much less success.

The majority of companies, however, continued to let small groups of leaders make choices, set our step-by-step guide of what to do ahead of us, and build great big machines to make sure everyone follows the steps. Is it because we found out new information that invalidated what our business gurus of the day were proposing? Do we see a new light in the data? Is the markedly successful reinvention of a company like Microsoft just too underwhelming? Or is it just too different and too difficult to lose control?

Losing control to gain engagement

Why do we love control? Because I believe we do love it, just listen to our language. Consider a phrase like, "They're out of control!" Unless you are 17 years old and talking to your friends about that one really cool but kind of rebellious person you all know, this is usually not considered a good thing. Taking control of a situation is an adult thing, it is seen as a needed thing. "It's under control" are reassuring words to hear. Now, calling someone a control freak is not usually a compliment, nor is saying they are controlling. So, used as an adjective (most often when used to describe others) control may be less positive, but as a noun it is generally considered good and useful.

David Rock, an author and lecturer in the relatively new field of "neuroleadership," which attempts to marry together neuroscience and leadership, created a core model for the neuroscientific underpinnings of human behavior in 2008 with his SCARF model.[2] While neuroleadership has its detractors, there has also been significant practical application and evolutionary biological support for some of its tenets. The SCARF model is particularly useful, in my experience. SCARF is an acronym that stands for **Status, Certainty, Autonomy, Relatedness,** and **Fairness.** In Rock's theory, these five things can be triggered, positively and negatively, in nanoseconds—and their triggering has consequences in our ensuing behaviors and relationships.

I would summarize my understanding of it this way. If I positively trigger you, by saying or doing things that raise your sense of status (Status) or help you understand what will happen next (Certainty) or ensure you have choice (Autonomy), then you will see me more favorably and begin to approach me with a positive confirmation bias. If I trigger you negatively, by shaming you (Status) or taking away your choices (Autonomy), or treating you in a way that you deem unfair (Fairness), then you will see me in a less favorable way and draw back from me, seeing me with negative confirmation bias.

My friend Mark Bowden would say that it is these reptilian brain stem-level reactions that lie at the heart of the need for control, and why it can be a good thing to relinquish it. If we are in control, our sense of what is coming next is increased (Certainty). We also are then comfortable that we get to choose what happens (Autonomy) and we are looked up to as those who have the power to make the choices (Status). We also know our place in the pecking order

(Relatedness) and are unlikely to feel treated unfairly since we control what is happening (Fairness). The desire for control is, therefore, completely natural. Having control is quite likely a product of our evolution as those of us with it did better in the natural selection process. So, the question is not really "Why would we want to have control?" so much as "Why *wouldn't* we want control, and why would we give it up?"

The giving up of our control is destabilizing and feels unnatural (literally, to our lizard brain) and has past echoes in our DNA of dire consequences. Nonetheless, it is the mindful giving up of control that we need to do in order to adapt to the fast-moving, digitally driven world around us. Why is that?

First of all, especially in a hierarchical organization, when we give up control (and all the comforts it brings) we give control to others. This can cause them to feel better in the same way it causes us, at least initially, to feel worse. But that is not the end of the story. If we use SCARF as a way of looking at control, we actually see that what we are looking for is to feel safe—to believe that we are out of harm's way. Or, at least, harm that we do not understand or cannot predict.

I believe that one of the reasons we have let hierarchy reign, despite the proven value of more distributed control, is that it is predictable for us. It may not always be pleasant or empowering, but at least we know the rules and where we stand. The hierarchy actually pushes a lot of SCARF buttons in a positive way. While some may be above us, there are (usually) also some below us, and we all either believe or desire to move up the ladder (Status). We have a good sense of who's who in the zoo (Relatedness) and while we might not like all the rules, and might even find them a bit unfair, we also see an equanimity in the fact that they are consistent (Fairness). Our choices may be limited, but within those limits we do have choices (Autonomy) and, therefore, we know what is coming. We may not always like the playing field, but we have accepted that the game is fairer than it is rigged. Others may have built-in advantages, but we know what they are, and we can also do our best to gain advantage for ourselves. Yes, it is a bit strange to say, but within the SCARF-negative atmosphere of the hierarchy we have found a way to make it into something positive for our little lizard brain and to believe that we can survive this particular jungle now that we know where the sabre tooth tigers are living.

Contrast that with suddenly being given power and control if we have not had it before. We've seen how it goes for the big bosses. One day they are on top of the world, the next day they are out, ignominiously and with the loss of significantly more income than we are making, and publicly. We've seen that the closer you get to the top, the greater the risks that come with those outsized rewards. And we have seen that the hierarchy always has a justification for the expulsions made. It was once the case that the decisions of the recently departed senior leader were universally lauded (at least out loud) and now they are universally decried (at least out loud) and those leaders no longer have a voice or any power in the organization.

Sudden redistribution of control can be quite SCARF-negative. If that control is distributed to you it may raise your status suddenly, in the formal hierarchy, but you may now find that you are suddenly a small fish in a big, murky new pond, instead of the bigger fish you were before. Even if your previous pond was less glamorous, it was clear water, and you knew where the predators were.

So, status can be mixed. And the new pond usually has new fish to deal with and you have no idea which ones have teeth and how they use them. Your ability to know what is coming next (Certainty) or know who the new fish are to you and what the nature of your relationship is to them (Relatedness) is now a problem. You may now have the authority to make choices (Autonomy) but this has actually been thrust upon you, it was not your choice, and suddenly you find that being forced to make choices is not autonomy at all.

As a senior leader I have watched many teams struggle when given control. I have seen them consistently complain about what leadership is doing but then get very unsure and uncomfortable when leadership relinquishes control to them. I have heard said, by very smart and good people, that their leader's decisions and direction were lacking. But when that same leader asked them to set the direction, they were also told that this was not their job, after all they were not the leader. Being able to criticize without having to solve the issue is a great place for the reptilian brain to be.

Please don't misunderstand, I am not being cynical and saying that employees are just whiners who are afraid to take leadership. That misguided line of thinking has helped leaders justify some less than empathetic or savory actions far too often. What I am saying is that both giving up control and getting control are not simple or easy exercises. There has to be a collaborative transition that is actively engaged in by both sides of the human equation for it to take hold and come to make a difference.

So how do we make it so that giving away control causes an increase in engagement, both for those of us giving it and those getting it? Well, if what our reptilian brain is looking for is to keep us alive, then we need to believe that this shift in control is safe.

Much has been written about psychological safety in recent years. It is well documented how Google's work to understand what makes effective teams and how to increase productivity and impact has been driven by increasing psychological safety.[3] Amy Edmondson, an American scholar of leadership, teaming, and organizational learning at Harvard, describes how the need for psychological safety has arisen as a "growing reliance on teams in changing and uncertain organizational environments creates a managerial imperative to understand the factors that enable team learning."[4]

Psychological safety is defined in a number of ways, but I think the most useful description I have read is from Timothy R Clark, "Psychological safety is about removing fear from human interaction and replacing it with respect and permission."[5] After all, how better to describe feeling safe as the absence of fear? How, then, do we give away (and get) control without causing fear? We have to do it specifically; with intent, purpose, and agreement—respect and permission.

We started by talking about clear, values-based purpose, and a man whose leadership resulted in an organization where "conversations for possibility replaced water cooler gossip," and "where meritocracy reined over hierarchy," through the vision and values he articulated. What I learned working with leaders like Ron Oberlander and Jean-Claude Casavant was that purpose was not enough. You had to have great intentionality and you had to work very hard to gain alignment about how your purpose and values would manifest.

When I was hired to lead Human Resource (HR) and Organizational Development (OD) for Abitibi-Price Sales Corporation, it was not because they could not manage the technical and transactional aspects of HR. It was because this was the last part of the organization to go through a very specific, well-planned, transformation. My key role was to support the president, C Don Martin, with his newly formed leadership team. Abitibi had become crystal clear on their vision and the values, as mentioned earlier—now they were putting them into action. To do that they had created a leadership group whose professional fates were inextricably linked. To combat the constant clash between sales and manufacturing, they had created business unit co-leaders from these two key business areas. These co-leaders had mostly separate responsibilities but shared all rewards. Their compensation was adjusted so that it was the same, to the penny. Their goals we equally shared and at the end of the year they received exactly the same variable rewards as each other, based upon their collaborative success against these cumulative goals. One could not succeed without the other. It was brilliant in its simplicity and I still marvel that I have not seen it in place elsewhere since.

The next step was to bring in someone who would not be focused on what the team was doing but on how they did it. Don specifically asked me to hold the team accountable to living the vision and values out loud. And, at Abitibi, this was not a gentle art. They had worked hard to engage in healthy conflict and to confront inconsistencies head on. "Straight talk" and the eschewing of "background conversations" were the phrases of the day. My job was to point out when this was not happening. Fortunately, I was too young and naive to realize how dangerous a role that could have been. Even more fortunate was the fact that the organization actually meant what they said and that I was backed up 110 percent when I pointed out where people were falling short. Here is an example of what might be said in a leadership meeting. "Does anyone here have a problem with the fact that none of you trust what Joe is saying and that, moreover, no one has spoken up to say what you are all thinking?" That quote (with the name changed to protect the guilty) is one I didn't have to seek permission to reprint, it was mine. I didn't say it with superiority or rancor, I said it with caring but directness. The leadership of the organization made me not only feel safe to speak this directly but valued for doing so. How? By explicitly creating a social contract that this was my role. No one was surprised. It was clearly stated that my role, in the leadership meetings, was to call the team out when we were not truthful or were avoiding difficult issues.

Even more importantly, after an interaction like that, it was most likely I would be thanked for the intervention—more often than not by the "Joe" of the day, and thanked publicly in front of the group. Because "Joe" was working just as hard as everyone to live by the vision and values and had just slipped up and back into old ways. He was not punished, he was not shamed, he was reminded, and corrected by the group with empathy. Sooner or later, everyone took their turn in the Joe box!

Respect and permission. It was at the core of everything and created an environment safe enough to cause the conflict that was required to perform at the highest level. Respect that we all make mistakes, and we all have each other's backs. Permission to say the hard thing someone needs to hear and to hold ourselves accountable to our commitments. It was one of the most rewarding roles I ever had, even when I took my turn in the Joe box. In fact, that may have been one of the most rewarding things because my own growth was real and immediate. There is a huge part of who I am today that was created in the loving crucible of Abitibi leadership meetings. However, I will say this: not everyone made it. Some leaders could not bear the scrutiny of their ideas or tolerate the conflict. They quickly opted out. Interestingly enough, even those thought to be critical contributors to success were really not missed and the impact of their departure was business accretive, not negative.

The five questions (plus one) of Pathfinding Before Path Following

We want to live and work in a world where we give respect and ask permission. A world where we make it safe to give and receive power and control. A world where we feel safe with that power and control. A world where we are guided by values and principles and these are what matter most, where the HiPPO (the Highest Paid Person's Opinion) is not the criteria for deciding all things.

How do we activate the behaviors of Pathfinding Before Path Following? Good question! As you know by now, the answer is… good questions! Here are the questions of Pathfinding Before Path Following. We will take each in turn, as usual.

> Question 1: Where are we really going?
> Question 2: What is most important?
> Question 3: Is this who we are?
> Question 4: Who would know best?
> Question 5: Can we discuss our differences?
> Bonus question: What am I hiding from you?

1. Where are we really going?

This is the fundamental question of pathfinding—**the destination question.** You must treat it with that same respect you are planning to treat others with and then give yourself, and your colleagues, permission to really ask the question. If you treat this one glibly and do not dig deep, you will end up with people who say they are headed in the same direction but who are actually not. This makes pathfinding very difficult, if not impossible, and will be almost certain to cause conflict of the not-so-useful variety as well as the misunderstanding that rots below the surface. "Where are we really going?" is how we get clarity on our destination, the one that we apply our values and principles to get to. The key to "Where are we really going?" is the word *"really."* Stress it, ask it again. This is the modifier that changes everything. You need to seek deep alignment on this.

That probably means that the words in the answer are all loaded with meaning specific to the culture they are in. Meaning that sits below the surface and must be explained and, much more importantly, role modeled to those new to the organization and to each other every day.

Here is an example. I said that the Abitibi-Price vision was "To be the world's finest manufacturer and marketer of paper for communication." Now, to be honest, when you read that do you get all excited? I didn't. But let me explore one word and help you understand what I came to understand about it. That word is "Finest." "Finest" was loaded with meaning. "Finest" did mean being financially successful, yes, but it didn't necessarily mean biggest. That would be great, but we would not sacrifice our values to get there. "Finest" meant responsibly, ethically and environmentally sound. "Finest" meant there was a certain elegance to how we operated and to how we treated each other (with respect and permission and truth). We could see "finest" behavior every day and know what it was and what it wasn't. We talked about it. "Does that make us the finest?" was a question that we could ask and explore and, more importantly, refine what "finest" meant to us in this moment. In this way the canon of what defined "finest" was built, person by person, and it gave depth and clarity to where we were *really* going.

2. What is most important?

This is the **values question**. While your company may have some stated principles or values that does not mean you are guided by them or that they are held as most important in making choices. The Scheins say that the three levels of culture are artifacts, stated values, and tacit assumptions.[6] Artifacts are those things you see on the surface. How do we dress, what does the workplace look like, what is the level of formality? In the past decade we have tried, in many companies, to adopt the culture of other successful companies, by emulating their artifacts. Nonetheless, I think we have all seen that just offering free snacks and lunch does not make us Google. Being frugal and avoiding expensive furniture and fancy office settings does not make us Amazon. Yet, because we can see them, we far too often land on artifactual changes as key to changing our culture. We have spent millions of dollars putting cultural lipstick on the corporate pig and, generally, the only thing it has done is make it clear to our people that we just don't get it.

Stated values are just what they seem, they are what we *say* we value. We will talk about who we say we are in the next question, but just know this about stated values—just because we say something is what we value doesn't make it true. Where stated values are critical is in how they align to our tacit assumptions. If they do not, we have a problem. If they do, we have a strong culture. So, while the obvious answer to "What is most important?" can be our stated values, we have to make sure. "What is most important?" is the question meant to dig into tacit assumptions. Tacit—understood or implied without being stated—means that these are the things we truly believe about "how things work around here." Tacit assumptions in action, this is truly culture. Artifacts and stated values play primarily in understanding if we can see ourselves clearly or if we cannot. Organizational self-awareness happens when we see, and talk about, how all three of these cultural elements align and when we make sure that tacit assumptions drive the others.

3. Is this who we are?

You might be thinking, "Hold on, how is this really different from 'What is most important?'" I like how you are thinking. "Is this who we are?" is **the accountability question**. The difference is that one explores our stated values as a company and the other explores our personal, individual challenges to ourselves and each other to live those values. It is how we look at our behaviors and choices and hold them up to the light of "What is most important?" "Where are we *really* going?" sets our North Star for us and "What is most important?" tells us what guides our feet as we choose from the many possible paths. "Is this who we are?" is where we pause, breathe, and make sure we have not started to march on without everyone, and anyone, being able to confirm that we are still heading toward our destination in the way we have determined it is best to move. It is how we ensure we are holding ourselves accountable to destination and values and how we continue to uncover how tacit assumptions manifest and how we keep our stated values aligned to those tacit assumptions. Because, while it happens slowly, if we are always holding ourselves accountable and exploring how our tacit assumptions show up, we will find that those assumptions can (and should) evolve over time. The world is full of corporate cultures that were exactly what worked once and now are killing that same company slowly and painfully. We become like the person who does not know they are slowly dying so they just wonder why they feel worse and worse each day, but don't do anything about it. After all, it's just the way it is.

When we are making choices daily, they should be based in "Where are we going?" and "What is most important?" And when we think we have made that choice and started moving, we should be looking at what that path now looks like and asking, "Is this who we are?" While the other two are at the highest level, this question is at the daily tactical level. Does what we are doing still look like it aligns to our destination and values or have we missed something or become lax? "Is this who we are?" provides us with diligence as we move forward.

4. Who would know best?

This is the **validation question**. This is how we ask for help, to make sure we are not straying from the principles and questions we use to find our path. This does not mean we are abdicating our responsibility to choose; it means we are getting help to see ourselves, and our actions, through the eyes of others who might have particularly keen sight. If "Is this who we are?" is the question where we hold ourselves accountable, "Who would know best?" is how we make sure we didn't miss something or not have enough information to make a good choice.

In my first executive role where the number of people I was leading became too big to work with each personally, I realized that I could not, and indeed should not, be making all the choices. Moving from being the decider to the leader is a pivotal moment in the leadership journey. It is one that some get stuck at and never truly progress further as a leader regardless of promotions. How do I stop making the decisions that I think demonstrate my value and that put me in the place of being the decision maker? How do I give up the control? What I hit upon, eventually, was that I needed a new social contract with the managers and leaders who reported to me in the organizational structure, one that passed on that control in a way that was safe for the recipient and myself. One where I was not making the choices but was also not flying blind, ignorant of the choices being made. Choices that I would, in the end, be held responsible for.

My social contract became simply this: I told my leaders that they were free to make the choices in their areas of responsibility without getting my permission or seeking my approval. I trusted them. That said, there were three things that might cause them to choose to tell me what they had chosen to do before acting. First, did they think it was possible or likely that I had information that, should they have it, might change their choice? If they were unsure, they should ask me. Not in order for me to second-guess their choices or potential choices, but so that I could provide them with all the information they needed to make their best choice. Second, might they need some "air cover" if the choice they were going to make would potentially run into opposition or cause conflict that we would be best to manage before the fact? If so, I was there to help them do this. That would, of course, also make sure I knew what was happening as it happened and could not only help them manage it, but also represent them, and their thought processes in the best light. Finally, this helped me to take on the mantle of responsibility for their choices as the leader who put them in their roles. The simple fact is that I was the one who met regularly with more senior leaders and it was likely I could smooth over conflict based on my deeper relationships. This was my job—to give them the space to do theirs.

So, in this way, I moved from being someone who told them what to do to a resource. I was a "Who would know best?" person they could count on to give them information, support them, and let them lead. Of course, a "Who would know best?" person does not have to be, and often is not, the person you work for. They can be a peer, they can be someone on your team, they can be the person who pours the tea. It doesn't matter who they are, as long as they can help you validate your course through perspective, expertise, and support.

5. Can we discuss our differences?

This is the **permission question**. Specifically, it is the question we use to obtain permission to disagree, to have conflict, to have the awkward conversation that, if we avoid it, will harm us. Human beings generally do not like conflict. Not only do we avoid it, especially at work, we are not good at it. Since conflict immediately makes things feel unsafe, we eschew it when we can, sometimes elaborately. But healthy conflict is how we actually sort out which choice is the best one at the time, and how we determine when that choice is no longer a useful one and we have to let it go. We need to give each other permission to disagree and then we need to get good at it. This is, for the vast majority of us, a journey. We do not flip a switch; our reptilian brain overrides our neocortex constantly. Embracing conflict is a learned skill.

In my work, I have used a simplified version of non-violent communication (NVC) by Marshall Rosenberg to help people embrace conflict and get better at it.[7] I won't teach NVC here but suffice it to say that it is about finding the real data or facts in a situation, not clouding them with your judgments (which look just like facts to you when you say them) and then getting really clear on what you want or need and then asking for it. We can leverage language from transactional analysis and say that an adult-to-adult relationship is marked by "Asking for what you want, knowing the answer may be 'no'." This is a great phrase to lead and live by.

But using any of these tools or ways of communication is predicated on getting permission to do so. "Can we discuss our differences?" does a number of things. First, it asks permission. This may not be a good time and place for that person, and that's okay. You need to then determine when you can discuss your differences, you can't just let it go, but you do have the option to step back for a bit. Second, it says "discuss." This is not "Can I tell you just how wrong you are?" which is not actually a question at all but a judgment, and not a flattering one. Third, it makes clear that there is no foregone conclusion here, there are differences. You are not saying, "Can we discuss how you are wrong?" We are being open to either or neither of you being right. But you are making clear that there are differences that need to be discussed. Finally, this is not about the people, it is about the issue at hand. You are not saying that they as a person are wrong, you are saying that what they think might be incorrect (as what you think might also be incorrect) and you want to partner with them to develop clarity and alignment.

So, one last thing. You have to be truly curious about this question when you ask it. In fact, you need to be truly curious with all of the questions in this book. When working with clients I will often tell them that the judgments they quickly think of or spit out that takes the form of a question are often the exact questions they need *if only they were truly questions and not judgments pretending to be questions*. Here is an example. Let's say I do something, and your immediate thought is "What are you thinking?" Hear yourself saying this question. In fact, right now, say it out loud. But, when you do, say it with all the scorn that belies the fact this this is not a question, this is a judgment, and the judgment is something along the lines of "You're not thinking at all!" Or maybe "You must be an idiot!" You know these types of questions; we have all been party to them on both giving and receiving. Now, strip away all the judgment and get really curious. Assume that I am smart, capable, and share your values and direction. Assume that I am a good person and that you care about me. Now, say it out loud again. "What are you thinking?" This question now becomes one that says, "I was not thinking that. I'm truly interested to know what your thought process is here. I respect you and want to either learn from you or help you learn. But, either way, we will understand each other better and be better off." This is an entirely different and much more productive conversation. A vastly superior one. But the words are exactly the same.

So, when you become cognizant that you have just formed a judgment masquerading as a question, stop, take a breath, get curious, get caring, and then truly ask the question as a question from a heart of transformation.

6. Bonus question—what am I hiding from you?

"What am I hiding from you?" is the **self-awareness question** that you ask yourself. It's not real fun to ask. But if you truly want to grow as a person, a colleague, and a leader, it is wonderful medicine, if a little hard to swallow. When you are in a pathfinding dialogue with another, you might start to feel that little twinge inside. You know the one. It is a vague sense that something is wrong or off. It is caused by hiding, when you are acting incongruently with what you believe your body tells you. Just think back to a time you lied to someone and remember that feeling in your stomach. I bet you are feeling it right now. That is a good indicator that you need to ask yourself this question. I am not advocating for you to always tell others what you are hiding. There may be valid reason not to. But there is also a great likelihood that you are protecting yourself, or think you are, from something you fear. This requires exploring. Where there is fear, there is growth. This question can help you find the fear and, therefore, find what you need to do next. One final thing about hiding. Research by Kegan and Laskow Lahey demonstrates that it is an incredible drag on productivity and results, not just a bad habit. Don't take it lightly, take it seriously![8]

Endnotes

1 Nadella, S (2019) *Hit Refresh: The quest to rediscover Microsoft's soul and imagine a better future for everyone*, HarperBusiness, New York

2 Rock, D (2008) SCARF: A brain-based model for collaborating with and influencing others, *Neuroleadership Journal*, **1** (1)

3 Duhigg, C (2017) *Smarter Faster Better: The transformative power of real productivity*, Random House, New York

4 Edmondson, A (1999) Psychological Safety and Learning Behavior in Work Teams, *Administrative Science Quarterly*, **44** (2), pp 350–83

5 Clark, T R (2020) *The 4 Stages of Psychological Safety: Defining the path to inclusion and innovation*, Berrett-Koehler Publishers, Inc., Oakland CA

6 Schein, E H and Schein, P (2017) *Organizational Culture and Leadership*, 5th edn, Wiley, Hoboken NJ

7 Rosenberg, M B (2015) *Nonviolent Communication: A language of life*, Puddledancer Press, Encinitas, CA

8 Kegan, R, Laskow Lahey, L, Miller, M L, Fleming, A, and Helsing, D (2016) *An Everyone Culture Becoming a Deliberately Developmental Organization*, Harvard Business Review Press, Boston MA

08

Innovating Before Replicating

A story of innovating

Innovating. It sounds exciting, it sounds like what everyone wants to do. It sounds like the future. But it is not the norm. Clay Christensen helps us understand this in his groundbreaking book *The Innovator's Dilemma*, which explains why companies fail at innovation time and time again. But being innovative in how we look at the world, and work, is at the core of building a heart of transformation. I will expand on that in a moment. But first, I would like to tell you a story of Innovating Before Replicating.

I've already introduced you to my friend and partner-in-crime Bob Moesta when we talked about Learning Before Knowing. What you don't know about Bob is that he has innovated literally thousands of products, many of which touch your lives every day. (That little arrow on your car dashboard that tells you which side the gas cap is on? Thank Bob). But, the story I am going to tell you is about a startup that he was a part of and how valuing Innovating Before Replicating changed everything for this company.

In 1998, Bob was a part of a startup company that made countertops, like the kind you have in a kitchen or bathroom. Countertops come in roughly three categories, from most basic to most extravagant: laminate, manufactured materials like Corian, and natural stone such as granite or marble. Bob's company made and sold a solid surface material Corian-like substance bonded to polymer concrete. While this was a new technology, in the end it was not the technology that proved to be the breakthrough.

The company had begun manufacturing and selling their counter-tops, but they were not growing like they wanted. When Bob got involved, the company had a strategy to be at parity with Corian but have other features, like increased durability. So, they set out to basi-cally replicate what Corian already sold successfully. They had 64 different colors and different types of edges and went head-to-head in the marketplace with the established leader. Not losing, but not winning big either.

Bob, one of the founders of Jobs-to-be-Done theory, began to look not at the product, but at the buyer. What did they really want? What progress were they trying to make in buying a product like this one? He discovered a few things. One was that the buying was directional; people were buying up from laminate, not down from stone. This meant that the company did not have to invest resources to compete with stone, just laminate. Second, while people would say that they wanted lots of color choices, they really did not distinguish between the eight shades of beige available. If only given the choice of one tone of beige, they would buy it. These people wanted something that looked better and lasted longer than laminate but, when it came to the decision of actually buying, color choice and features were not near as important as cost and availability.

Having learned this, Bob set out to shake things up. First, he took them down to eight colors. People said to him, "You can't do that!" He also decided to make them modular and not custom, as was industry standard, to which people said, "You can't do that!" But, at the cost point of the product, it seemed he could do that. Sales began to grow.

But he wasn't done. One of the problems with the manufacturing is that there are seams where the product pieces fit together. Try as they might, they could not get perfect seams that lined up flawlessly. This cost them time and materials to try to fix. So instead of solving the problem, Bob accentuated it; he made it a feature. They began to manufacture with very noticeable seams in the product that were connected by the much more forgiving grout-like material that stuck them together. Problem solved. But people said (you guessed it), "You can't do that!" But, interestingly, producers of natural stone countertops did that. The new "feature" actually mimicked that of the higher-value product. Remember, people were moving up from laminate so that was a "feature" that had not been available to them before.

Sales took off and were greatly simplified since they only offered eight colors, visible seams, and modular pieces. In a few short years they grew the company nearly 20 times in revenue and finally sold it when they had started to grow so fast that they were running out of cash to fund the incredible increase in volume to be manufactured.

What did they learn about Innovating Before Replicating? First, that conventional wisdom is not always very wise. Long-established norms or beliefs in the industry (range of color, visible seams, customization) were taken for granted as true, but they didn't matter to the customer who, in the end, was the one buying. They learned that you need to innovate and simplify before replicating or scaling. Seeing this allowed Bob's company to get to market faster. Competitors who were still customizing just pushed out product lead times. Bob's company was able to beat them on delivery date every time.

Finally, they learned that buyers could not actually articulate what they wanted. When asked if they wanted color choice and customization, they said they did, but that is not what caused them to buy. Getting it faster and more easily did, even though people did not push for that or declare a need for that when buying.

In summing up some of this story, Bob said, "People (in business) spend all their time focusing on where the money comes from. They don't spend near enough time focusing on where the future comes from!" The future in this particular market was limited choice, limited size and shape, low-cost, and fast delivery. Bob and his team saw it and they took that foresight all the way to the bank.

It is not only startups that need to step away from replicating. Consider a company like IBM. Before the personal computer, they were a mainframe computing company. Mainframes were big and costly with high margins, around 40 percent. When the PC was considered, the mainframe leaders could not see why they would ever add in a product whose margins were likely to be more like 10 percent. That was going backwards! Or was it? Big companies struggle to do things of lower quality and/or less margin and so they see reducing the quality or margin ratios as a mistake. Disruptors see an increasingly low-end market as an opportunity. Bob paraphrased something that Clay Christensen used to say to him in their work together, "We should be measuring the pounds of cash, not the ratios of things."

In the end, that low margin, lower quality, and far less sophisticated PC proved to be a very good innovation indeed.

So, what is it about replicating (or scaling) that has such a hold on modern organizations? That's what we are going to explore next.

The replication religion

When writing this section, I turned to my friend Rob Wengel who, not uncoincidentally, was the person who introduced me to Bob Moesta. He has spent a career helping people understand why and how to innovate and truly understand the market they serve. His superpower is helping people step away from their prior successes to see that they are now hanging on to a product or service that is now ripe for disruption or is on the wane. I asked him why people get so attached to merely repeating and scaling past success. Because replicating or scaling success is not a wrong-headed strategy, it is a good one. Until it no longer is. (I am hoping you, gentle reader, will have started to see the pattern emerging—it is not that what came first, in this chapter *replicating*, is wrong, it is just that it is no longer enough and the new capability, *innovating* in this case, is what helps keep the old one honest).

Let's start with what this new product development is anchored in or driven by. According to Rob, these are:

1 The need to bring new news to the company, and especially your boss or shareholders or owners.

2 Chasing a trend that you believe is going to make an impact or will soon become the norm.

3   There is a demographic group or market segment that the company wants or strategically needs to have.

4   The company has the capability to develop the new product, so they decide not to waste that capability.

5   The competition is doing it, so I better do it too. Fear of missing out (FOMO) is a powerful force in business.

Not one of these things is inherently bad, but all of them carry risks and costs, and they are risks that are not certain of being overcome and costs that are not certain to be recouped upon or to deliver growth. This is where replication comes in. Replicating is simply easier because someone has already spent the time to identify the market and what would successfully meet those needs in the market (at least at a point in time). That someone might even have been from the organization itself and so that knowledge of the market and what would meet the needs represents money spent, a sunk cost that they want to get back, and then some. The fact of the matter is that replicating is simply easier than innovating.

But maybe the most wonderful and damning thing about replicating and scaling successful products is that it works. Once again, until it doesn't. Jeff Bezos is quoted as saying, "A company shouldn't get addicted to being shiny because shiny doesn't last."[1] Therein lies the problem with success, it never lasts. Unfortunately for successes, the world changes. The context shifts, others enter the market, technology happens, etc. Innovating and taking risk is, well, risky. The chance of failure is high. In fact, it is a certainty that some innovations will fail, maybe most. Sometimes you don't find that out until you have failed at scale, which can have significant cost. The great casino that is our capitalist system does not like to lose money. Moreover, it has a timetable for making money, which is driven by the utterly random, but completely institutionalized, practice of quarterly and annual returns. It has always fascinated me that the hard-working, inventive, passionate, driven, and creative people running companies are absolutely accepting of the timeframe boundaries we have set ourselves years ago. Of course, Wall Street is a major player in respecting the fences, and even putting more of them up. But that is not because they are dedicated to the success of any given company, it is because it helps them place their bets and control the rules of the table. Those who play the game get the spoils. Those who refuse to play by the rules get punished (at least most do, more on that in a minute). The punishments can be great: loss of status, loss of opportunity, loss of job, loss of livelihood, and many more. And that's scary. The fear of failure is real and deep–and we have created organizations that are perfectly designed to foment those fears.

As I have said, I believe that most human behavior can ultimately be explained by our matchless drive to avoid fear and shame. I know, it sounds a bit dark. And, yes, I agree that there are absolutely positive motivations for doing things as well. We have dreams, passions, desires, etc. But it is more often than not that our desire to avoid fear is more powerful than our drive to experience hope. In fact, why don't you go ahead and do a little internet search to see if you can find a consensus as to what is the opposite of fear. Some say hope, like I just used. Some say curiosity, others say calmness or confidence or something else. It is telling, in and of itself, that while we all agree fear sits on one side of the fence, we are unsure of what is on the other.

The costs and rewards of fearlessness

Okay, I realize that Amazon has not only become ubiquitous as a presence in near all of our lives but that it also has become the overwhelming example and metaphor in business to the point of oversaturation and fatigue. (For those of you in countries where Amazon is not king, there is a similar competitor of local origin which has learned quickly from the Amazon example that likely is the example usually cited.) Nonetheless, while we are very unlikely to create the "next Amazon," the rules that they play by do have lessons for us all. This is particularly true in Innovating Before Replicating. There are two particular aspects of Amazon that help drive innovating—learning from failing and playing the long game.

Jeff Bezos started the move to a public company with Amazon with an unusual pitch. He basically guaranteed his investors that he would commit to losing money for at least five years, maybe more. He was very clear that there would be no short-term gains, only cost. Profit did not matter, yet. What mattered was market share and learning what customers truly wanted and valued. To that end, he made big bets, some of which paid off so well that to describe that payoff as "handsome" would be one of the sillier understatements one could make. And he played a long game. Consider these words of his:

> I don't think that you can invent on behalf of customers unless you're willing to think long-term, because a lot of invention doesn't work. If you're going to invent, it means you're going to experiment, and if you're going to experiment, you're going to fail, and if you're going to fail, you have to think long term.[2]
>
> You need a culture that high-fives small and innovative ideas and senior executives [that] encourage ideas. In order for innovative ideas to bear fruit, companies need to be willing to wait for 5–7 years, and most companies don't take that time horizon.[3]

These are not, actually, hard ideas for us to reconcile in our heads as likely to be true. But they are very hard ideas to get our organizational cultures and rules to accept. Cultures that we created and rules that we choose to play by, mind you, but that we let get in our way, nonetheless. The example that Amazon set for us was that you could win, and win big, by changing the rules and building the organizational culture to support playing by those new rules we had set. Figuring out the new rules of trading short term for long-term thinking and measuring success differently, as well as putting your failing and learning machine in motion, is not truly hard. What is truly hard is creating the culture that not only accepts but embraces these new rules. That is something we create one person at a time.

Challenging assumptions with platform thinking

Before we move into the questions of Innovating Before Replicating, let's take a look at the power of our frame of reference. We go through the day making most of our choices without actually making them.

Wait, what?

Let me elucidate here as we have talked about assumptions already, but they are important enough to look at again. According to research by Duke University, 45 percent of what we do during a given day is done out of habit.[4] This is not a bad thing. Our brains cannot take the time to process every stimulus that enters our consciousness in an equal manner, it would make us crazy. Sensory gating, as it is called, helps us filter out the unimportant stimuli so we can use the (relatively) limited capacity of our neocortex on what matters. In fact, people with schizophrenia show a decreased sensory-gating capacity, for whom the disorientation of the flood of stimuli, non-differentiated, is not just unpleasant, it is debilitating.

A healthy brain does what it is supposed to do, it puts the "less important" or habitual or routine things "out of mind" so we can focus on what matters most. Or does it? The only way our brain can do that is by making assumptions about what matters most and then acting as if those assumptions were truth. And here is the interesting thing about those assumptions: most of them are true. Until they aren't. The assumptions we make are useful at a point in time. They fit the context of their creation. But time marches on and the world (and, therefore, our context) changes and those assumptions age, and not like a fine wine, more like unpreserved fruit. So how do we challenge our assumptions? We have talked about tackling assumptions head on by just asking ourselves, "What am I assuming is true?" and "Who challenges my beliefs?" but there is another way that assumptions are being challenged, and innovative thinking happening, and that is through platform thinking.

The technology idea of platforms (often productized as platform as a service, or PaaS) is simply the technology, or a group of technologies, on which other technology, such as applications or processes, are developed or based. In business speak, a platform is usually described as a model that creates value by facilitating exchanges between two or more interdependent groups, usually consumers and producers. In plain speak, a platform is the bigger thing in which the smaller things connect, reside, or interact. For our purposes of "platform thinking," it is the frame of reference in which our assumptions sit. Let's start with getting clearer on frame of reference. What is a frame of reference? Let's take a tasty approach to that question.

Consider the US versions of Snickers and Milky Way candy bars (if those are familiar to you and, if not, I think the explanation that follows will help). Unwrap a couple, cut them in half, and what do you see? Chocolate outside, nougat and caramel layered one on top of the other inside. They are virtually the same except for the addition of peanuts in the Snickers bar. But they solve completely different problems for their consumer, at least in how they are successfully marketed. And those problem sets are the frame of reference. Milky Way is marketed as a delicious indulgent treat. Therefore, it competes with ice cream, snack cakes, and even alcoholic drinks. It is oh-so-good and yummy. One recent ad campaign built upon this sentiment by showing traditional Milky Way bars with the words "Awesome" or "Oh My Gosh" next to them, followed by their new Milky Way Bites (a small, pop-in-your-mouth-sized version, sold in bags) with the words "Awe" and "OMG" next to them. Same great indulgence, smaller size, get it?

So how about Snickers? Don't they fill that same need of indulgent treat, just with the addition of crunchy, crispy peanuts? Nope. Snickers competes with hunger. What do they claim to do? A Snickers satisfies, right? That's the tagline anyone familiar with a Snickers bar knows well. They compete with temporary meal replacement; they fill the tummy quickly and easily. So, they compete with coffee, other bars like protein and meal replacement bars, even fruit. While these candy bars are virtually identical products, excepting the peanuts, they live in entirely different frames of reference. This has helped Mars not only sell an enormous amount of these products but it has also kept them from competing with each other so they can expand their markets. This is brilliant thinking on behalf of Mars. All too often, producers just see the product and then look to compete with other products in the same category, in this case by assuming they are interchangeable, and merely candy.

So now we know that the frame of reference can be bigger than we thought, let's look at what a platform perspective is. A platform is the place where we can connect the wider frames of reference. At Gartner we used to use an example we called the car crash scenario to explain this.

Imagine that Dick is taking Tommy and Tammy to school in the family minivan one morning and Jane (unrelated to Dick) is rushing to the office and attempts to beat that changing traffic signal. Unfortunately, the amber light becomes red before she can get past it and she and Dick have a collision. What happens next is really interesting. First, the smartphones in both Dick's and Jane's possession register the sudden decelerations that can only signal a collision. As a result, the MyCarCrash application on their phones leaps into action. It queries sensors in the clothing and smart wearables of all four of them to determine what their health status is. Is there blood? Are they breathing? Is an ambulance needed and needed immediately or are their injuries limited or non-life-threatening? This inquiry triggers the appropriate calls to hospitals and first responders, so they not only know to come to the scene, but what they need to be prepared for and how serious the situation is. The app also queries the onboard computers in their cars to see how extensive the damage is. Will the jaws of life be needed to extricate any of them? Will their cars need to be towed or can they be driven to where they can be repaired? And what about those repairs? The app connects to the systems of local body shops and looks at the calendars of Dick and Jane. It negotiates the best rate and schedules the appointment to drop off the car when it best fits the schedules of the owners.

Fortunately, the accident is not fatal, it's more in the fender-bender category. But Tommy and Tammy are definitely going to be late for school and Jane will miss that morning meeting she was so eager to get to. So, the app notifies the school that the kids will be approximately 90 minutes late, given the time it will take to get through the police reporting and then dealing with growing traffic congestion along the route. Jane's clients are notified, and their meeting is rescheduled to an available slot for everyone later that week, after a less important meeting of Jane's is rescheduled, since the app has connected with her smart calendar that knows what her priorities are. Dick's wife is notified as well via Instagram (or Facebook, or

Twitter, etc.) and she sees a quick video of the kids smiling and okay. Finally, the footage from cameras near the scene is collected and sent to the insurance companies and attorneys so that the fault and payment can be sorted out.

All of this happens in a matter of moments. It involves multiple technologies interfacing with myriad people and other technologies. Underlying all of that is the platform that made it possible, the place where all the applications and processes are connected and upon which the MyCarCrash app was built. This platform has taken care of so many things at once that the fee charged for its use is a no-brainer. A business has been born. None of what was done could not have happened independently and, in fact, the providers of technology, like the sensors in the clothing or the social media platforms used, do operate independently. But the platform pulls them all together to create an entirely new stream of revenue.

The MyCarCrash app and platform does not exist, at least not yet. But the technology is here and it is now just a matter of cost, something that is always decreasing with technology.

I share all of this to say that if you want to live in a world of innovating over replicating, context or frame of reference and platform thinking is a must.

The five questions of Innovating Before Replicating

To activate an innovative mindset, we need to question our assumptions a little more deeply than we have, and we also need to examine the learning that comes particularly from getting it wrong.

Question 1: What have I learned from my failures?
Question 2: Do I have the stomach for the long game?
Question 3: What is the cost of replicating our success?
Question 4: How do I stop being the center of the universe?
Question 5: How would I disrupt me?

1. What have I learned from my failures?

This is the pivot question; it tells us how we use our failures. Do we use them to grow or just punish ourselves? "What have I learned from my failures?" is not a question with the sole answer "nothing," except in two circumstances. One, you are actually a mythic deity. Two, you haven't learned to learn from your failures. To avoid the latter (because the former does not apply to me), I tend to use this question a little differently and I keep a list of answers to it. This list becomes the foundation of what I know about me to be true and to help me develop the cognitive triggers to see myself more clearly and become aware when I am letting my assumption-loving brain have free rein to live a less examined life. Seeing the patterns in our failures helps us avoid making those same mistakes as often.

From the patterns of my failures, I have learned the following about myself:

- I like to be liked—this may sound silly at first, but it can be debilitating, especially when my role is to challenge or drive healthy conflict. If I give in to this need, I can blunt my effectiveness as a coach, consultant, and leader. As a result, I try to care enough to say what I believe even when it does cause conflict, and I trust that I'll be liked enough in life and decide that I would rather be effective than liked, if I cannot have both.

- I like to be right—and this one has cost me time and time again. There are few things worse than being the person with the answer only to find out you have lost the ears of your audience and you are now raging against the nothingness. In most cases, it is far less useful to be right and far more useful to make progress, especially if it is made in collaboration with others. As a result, I ask others to help me see where I am wrong, or only partially right, etc. I work hard to remain open to my inevitable fallibility and to invite others in to challenge me and reward or thank them for doing so.

- I like to be smart—there have been so many times where I have realized that I was expounding, explaining, and pontificating and that the only thing the people unfortunate enough to be in earshot were learning was how much I thought I knew. Sometimes I did know a lot, and a lot more than them, which didn't help them learn, it just helped them assume that I thought less of them. Not a winning formula for collaboration and partnership. As a result, I tend to listen more. This is hard for me as I am definitely a talker! One simple hack that a coach of mine gave me for when I was going to be walking into a situation where my anxiety was likely to cause me to talk more, and therefore listen less, was just simply to talk 50 percent less. Of course, there is no way to measure this, but just making the effort to approximate 50 percent less talking than normal is a huge help. I will never forget the first time I followed this advice and it completely turned around a relationship. I was shocked at how something so simple could be so powerful.

I could go on here, but I think you get the point. The value in "What have I learned from my failures?" is not to catalogue those failures but to learn; to see the patterns, know your own personal tripwires, and develop strategies to overcome or manage those tripwires.

2. Do I have the stomach for the long game?

This is the **fortitude question**. It's true that we cannot all be Jeff Bezos, but we can reset our mind for the longer game. Make no mistake, there are a number of forces aligned up against us in playing the longer game. First, our metrics in most companies are short-term. It is possible to change those metrics, but there are a lot of powerful stakeholders that benefit from keeping them the way they are. Especially those stakeholders that benefit in the short term from investment returns and variable compensation. If you are going to play the long game, you need to take a good hard look at who benefits from playing the short game. To play a long game, you need to set goals that don't pay off early on, or at all as a discrete goal, but that demonstrate progress toward the long-game goal. You can do this in business, and you can do this personally.

Take this book, for example. You are holding in your hand one of those very goals that doesn't pay off for its author in the short term, and there is no guarantee it will pay off in the long term, but it does show progress. I will not make much money from selling this book unless it becomes a wild bestseller. To that end, I strongly encourage you to buy a few boxes to have on hand to give to friends, share on social media how it changed your life, and buy the T-shirt! Okay, just kidding (although it does make a good gift, I'm just sayin'). Writing this book, for me as a professional, is a part of playing a long game. What I hope for is a platform to get a message out there that I truly believe in. I am also hoping to develop business from the seeds that the book plants. If the ideas within this book inspire, motivate, or support the transformation of individuals and organizations, I will have more opportunities to do the same. That might come in the form of products that further operationalize the concepts, it might come in the form of opportunities to speak, it may come in as consulting and advising opportunities where I actually leverage my enterprise-wide, digitally enabled tools and services to drive wide-ranging organization transformation.

But I won't get there without starting with having something to say that makes a contribution and adds value to the reader of the book. It's a risk. I am risking time spent where I could be doing paid work. I am risking that my voice won't resonate or that the timing won't be right. But I believe in the long game in life and I know what I have the stomach for, so this is how I proceed. I have left the status and steady pay of executive corporate roles for the uncertainty of doing what I love to do most in the world—create spaces for others to step into and to become more than they thought they could be.

3. What's the cost of replicating our success?

This is the **dark-side question**. When we repeat what has worked, we don't often look at the costs. And the cost is not just that if you replicate you don't innovate, that's far too simple. And the costs are not always high, in fact there are clearly times of real benefit from best practices or scaling what is working. But we do want to know what we might be giving up even when the replicating is good. First, we may be giving up learning. That means we are not exercising our learning brain, which means that it is not getting stronger. And if that is true for us, it is even more true for our teams. Speaking of teams, we are teaching them to be executors, not explorers. When we are telling (to replicate what is working) instead of asking (what is different that we could do?) then you are making clear to them that their job is to do, not to dream—and there are a lot of minds out there that might have the dream you need in them.

Working with a global oil and gas company once, I had a discussion about this with their executive leadership team. We had just gone through an exercise that had shown them how hard they struggled to be creative and innovative (and use platform thinking) in this industry they were so intimately familiar with and immersed in. We discussed the culture and who was expected to have ideas, to think innovatively. We talked about how they actually encouraged (or didn't) their people to bring those ideas forth. And we realized that the odds were that the next breakthrough idea they might have was actually unlikely to come from that room of the most senior people in the company. We then pictured in our minds an employee. She was an African woman standing in her overalls and talking to a customer at the work site and we realized that she was going to see something that could change everything, maybe she was out there and already had. But, as leaders, they had done nothing that said to her that her ideas mattered, or that they would be listened to, or that the team even wanted them. The cost of replicating our success meant that we would never have all the other successes that might be out there.

4. How do I stop being the center of the universe?

This is the **step-back-and-see-myself** question. We need this question because, yes, that's how we all see it, like it or not, from our point of view. We respond to everything from our perspective, we filter everything through our experience. We are the norm (even though we are above average in most ways, right?). An innovative mindset requires us to put others at the center of the universe, even if only for a short time and a particular purpose. I could have asked, "How do I become customer obsessed?"—but I don't find that particularly helpful as a way to operationalize empathetic curiosity, it really just describes the outcome I am looking for in language that Amazon has made famous. It also implies that it is about them, the customer, but the harder part is that it is about my unspoken and unseen assumptions about me, that I am the center of truth. Until I recognize that, I will miss any number of things that I need to help me be more innovative in my approach, especially data that doesn't fit with my own worldview. The brain's ability to rationalize just about anything that reinforces our rightness is well documented, so we must learn to be a bit suspicious of ourselves.

5. How would I disrupt me?

This is the **changing-myself** question. Have you ever thought about your own, personal competitors? Kind of a weird idea, unless maybe you are gunning for a promotion, trying for a new job, or vying for the attention of someone you really dig but who has other admirers as well. It's actually something you will find very useful. Think about your work, what you do, how you do it, and then think about the person who could come in and displace you. What kind of person could make you irrelevant or old hat? What would they do that you are not doing?

When I think about this, here are some of the things that come to mind. I could be disrupted by someone with a bigger, bolder presence in the market. While I am well networked and have some powerful experiences and roles under my belt, I have not had much of a presence outside the circles I touch personally. Hopefully, as you read this, you think that's not true. I have engaged a partner to help me overcome this. It is a key investment that I make in myself and my business. My marketing mentor, Fei Wu at www.feisworld.com, not only works for me, but she works with me, and she makes me work harder and better. I need her push and discipline just as much as I need her experience, insight, and enthusiasm. Thinking about how to disrupt me was one of the things that led me to her.

I also realize that the person who could disrupt me would have more discipline than I do. I find it easy to procrastinate, I always have. I wrote this chapter and the next chapter in just a few short days while on a working vacation in Maine. Not because it was the right environment, but because I no longer had a choice. If I didn't get them in, I'd really be letting down my editor. I wished I'd blocked out more time to start writing earlier. You see, once I start writing, it goes fairly quickly and really starts to flow. The disruptor of me would remember that and then just have planned to start sooner and more frequently. We might both get the job done, but they would be less stressed and might even get more done. They would definitely make it go faster and easier.

For you, your disruptor might be very different. They might have acquired a skill you haven't, like how to use Python to do simple analytics. They might get up in front of the crowd and be willing to share what they know instead of hiding their light under a bushel. They might ask for that raise or charge more than you do, because they don't worry that they are not worth it. You will have to figure it out. Regardless of how you do it, find your disruptor in your head and then figure out what you are going to do with that knowledge. You want to be the person to disrupt you first, of that I am certain.

Learning from the best—the awesomeness of awkwardness

I first really began to think about the value of awkwardness when working with Robbe Richman and Daniel Mezick. They had shot a brief video for us when my team at GE was trying to help our organization understand and embrace the ways of working in a digital world. In the video they are talking about Agile. We wanted people to step away from the process and look at the intent and how that was reflected in people and not the process. Dan was discussing the kind of very real and confrontative conversation that good Agile teams had about what did, and didn't, get done. He talked about how that kind of direct questioning and honesty did not reflect the face-saving norms of most companies when he said, "If it isn't awkward, it isn't Agile!"

There is so much value in that little phrase. Not just for Agile teams, but for all of us. Dan was not warning us against creating awkwardness, he was warning us against avoiding it! For a group to align, some people need to change their views or acknowledge the usefulness of views they don't hold, and act accordingly. To do that, you need to surface the differences. You need to have conflict. Sometimes it seems as if there are only two kinds of people when it comes to conflict in our organizations. The first is the majority group who desperately avoid conflict. The second is the minority group who use it to show dominance or power over others. But conflict has a higher purpose. It surfaces the problems that we would otherwise deny or avoid, but that exist all the same. It helps us understand and appreciate the differences between ourselves and others. This helps us build empathy. It might help us see ourselves through the eyes of others and, therefore, more clearly. Finally, it provides us that opportunity to break old and ineffective habits or patterns that no longer serve us well. Conflict is not about resolution; it is much more often about management—uncovering and making choices that will actually be implemented.

Tools for transformation—turning awkward into forward

Awkwardness is the harbinger of conflict, and that is a good thing. When you see it, do you pay attention? When you are about to create it, think about the purpose it will serve. When it is over, think back on how it truly felt. In the end, would the apprehension of the awkward moment have been worth missing what happened, what you uncovered, what you did?

So, when things are about to get a little awkward in the search for truth, here are some ideas to help you move through it to the other side where progress and clarity awaits.

1 When something you are about to say or ask is likely going to make things a bit awkward then just hide in plain sight. Say, "What

I am about to say might make things a bit awkward, but we'll be okay." Then say it. That tiny embedded command of a social contract can give you both the permission you need to step into awkwardness and then pass through it with your relationship intact.

2   Thank people for engaging in the awkward moment. A phrase like, "I know that was kind of awkward for both of us, but I really appreciate you helping me understand what is really happening," can bring the relational closeness back that we fear awkwardness might cost us. Reward and reinforce others for engaging in awkward with you.

3   Laugh. Sometimes you just need to take the awkward that has reared its head and put it square in the middle of the room. You don't rescue it, you don't excuse it, you just acknowledge, "That was kind of awkward!" and break the tension with laughter. It doesn't mean it wasn't awkward, but it does indicate that awkward is not fatal.

4   Give yourself, and others, a safe way to say the awkward thing. Way back in my days working for Abitibi-Price, we had this wonderful consultant who would bring a small stuffed moose toy to our meetings. In Canada, what I have heard Americans call acknowledging "the elephant in the room," was referred to as "putting the moose on the table." After all, there are more moose in Canada than elephants. She would bring in this little stuffed moose toy and when someone realized the thing that needed to be said was not being said they would ask for the moose and would literally put it on the table. Then they would say what needed saying. This simple tool worked brilliantly. Just bringing the moose in gave us agreed permission to say the awkward thing. The act of putting it on the table signaled what was about to happen and told us that we needed to really listen and be prepared to hear, not defend. This was a moment to see what we could learn. These days I have several pairs of small stuffed animals that go with me to consulting engagements where awkwardness might be needed to surface the real problems. One, an elephant (unless I am in Canada)

that serves the same purpose as the moose. The other is a donkey. I tell the room that the donkey protects you and makes it safe to ask that question that you are afraid will make you look like… well… let's just say it's another word for donkey that has some definite negative connotations. I have seen senior leaders grab the donkey with a death grip as they spit out their "dumb" question, only to see them release it in relief when someone in the room both affirms that they had the same question and how useful a question it actually is. I'll never forget the first time I used this tool and saw that happen. It was in a group of about 25 leaders of equivalent stature. The leader who grabbed the donkey is the only one who has become a CEO. Coincidence? Maybe.

My advice to you is to embrace the awesomeness of awkward and find the truth and trust it ultimately brings. A heart of transformation is a bit messy, a little awkward, and richly rewarding.

Endnotes

1 Levy, S (2011) Jeff Bezos Owns the Web in More Ways Than You Think, *Wired* [online] http://www.wired.com/magazine/2011/11/ff_bezos/all/1 (archived at https://perma.cc/5DFX-C43C)

2 GeekWire (2013) Jeff Bezos Explains Why Amazon Doesn't Really Care About Its Competitors [online] https://www.geekwire.com/2013/interview-jeff-bezos-explains-amazon-focus-competitors/ (archived at https://perma.cc/9A7L-556L)

3 Malik, O (2009) Tips on Innovation & Entrepreneurship from Jeff Bezos [online] https://gigaom.com/2009/06/15/tips-on-innovation-enterprenuership-from-jeff-bezos/ (archived at https://perma.cc/UG5V-A458)

4 Neal, D T, Wood, W, and Quinn, J M (2006) Habits—A Repeat Performance, *Current Directions in Psychological Science*, **15** (4), pp 198–202

09

Humanizing Before Organizing

A story of humanizing

Jesse Davis is a true techie. But what defines him for me is his heart, because he is a human being first and his love of technology plays a clear second to his love of people. Jesse and I met when I was working with the company that is now called Devada, but better known for the brands of their platforms DZone and AnswerHub. DZone is the place where developers come together with other developers so they can learn from each other as they try to change the world through software. AnswerHub is the platform on which this work can be done, both externally as an open and public platform (like DZone) and internally as the platform where software engineers collaborate in some of the most successful technology companies on earth. You may not know this unless you are a software developer, but you might want to take note as they are greatly improving how work gets done together in this area of work that is changing the world the most.

Terry Waters, the CEO of the Devada companies, and I go back many years to early days at Gartner where he developed and led Gartner's C-suite advisory business, executive programs, and where I was his head of HR before leading an international region of executive programs and, eventually, innovating the division's products and services. When Terry became CEO at Devada, after a successful run leading several other companies, he asked me to work with him as an advisor and consultant as he developed the Devada business and culture into a market leader. Jesse, the former head of technology at the company, and one of the company's first employees, was also working on a consulting arrangement with Devada and we got to know each other through working together as fractional leaders in the company, working with Terry and the executive team. While we come from very different backgrounds, we found a connection immediately. If I had to give a reason for that, I think it would be just our shared love of the potential of others. We both are passionate about helping others be all that they can be and encouraging and stretching their thinking, self-perception, and the size of their dreams. He is also just a fun and funny guy and I appreciate that so much in a colleague. Finally, he is someone with whom I quickly was able to figure out how we could best support the purpose of a company we both believe in.

I have saved Humanizing Before Organizing as the last of the six capabilities to discuss because it is the one that, personally, means the most to me and informs who I am and what I do. I have myriad stories about this from my own experiences, but I wanted to find something about how others put Humanizing Before Organizing to drive great success. I had a hunch Jesse might have a story or two like that and so, during a call scheduled for another purpose, I ambushed him and said, "Tell me a story of why the relationships we have with people matter more than the roles they play," and he immediately rose to the challenge. This is the story he told me.

In 2012 he was working for a different technology company that was trying to make the move to software as a service (SaaS). SaaS is a nearly ubiquitous term now, even non-techies have heard it, and there are thousands of companies today which are SaaS and PaaS (platform as a service) companies. But a few short years ago, this was not the case. Cloud was new and limited and most companies sold software that was stored locally or on internal servers. The "everything in the cloud" world was being touted by few and strongly resisted or downplayed by many. It seems strange to think of that now, but it wasn't that long ago. Time moves differently in the digital age.

Jesse, the head of research and development at this company, was working to build the teams that would drive this small organization to create a true SaaS product through Agile methods and mindset. In this role, talent was everything. He knew what to do, but having the talent that could build it fast, first, and best, was the key to success.

I've been involved in the talent game for a long time. I've led the full lifecycle of talent—acquisition, management, development, transition, etc.—and I've consulted to dozens more companies, from the largest to the very small, on the same. There is a lot of "tried and true" wisdom out there. Much of this wisdom is, unfortunately, often overly tried and not actually very true at all. As for it being wisdom? Well, I'll leave it to you to look at what you have seen in this space and tell me. But if you have been through a frustratingly information- and humanity-free recruiting process, or some bland and boring learning and development process, or maybe a life-draining performance management process, and finally a humiliating and nearly inhuman "rightsizing" process in one or many companies, then you know my feeling on the state of Talent (with a capital T, not meaning the people themselves) in far too many companies.

Jesse was working at a smaller company at the time so he had a lot of freedom and a lack of bureaucracy, which meant he could basically do what he wanted to do, within the bounds of the law and his moral and ethical values. He must have done something right as that company was approaching half a billion US dollars in revenue as of 2020. So what Jesse did is he sat down and asked himself what it was that he was most looking for in the team that he needed to build and then lead through this difficult task of moving first, fast, and with excellence, and actually building a true SaaS company of a size that just didn't exist at that time. Remember, most "cloud" was internal to really big companies and just meant their collection of server farms. Amazon Web Services (AWS) was nowhere to be seen and Azure was the color of the sky, not something we all stored our PowerPoints on. Small companies did not operate as SaaS companies, they sold software in a box.

Jesse considered this question as he thought about the skills and technical capabilities needed in the talent he sought. Their education.

Their experience. Their certifications. And as he thought about all of these, he realized that there was actually only one thing that really mattered most. You could hire for all of the background, technical capabilities, experience, and certifications you wanted but, as Jesse said to me, "There's really only one, last true competitive differentiator in the world—being able to work together."

Now, that might sound fairly facile on the face of it, but it is actually quite profound and significant if we just pause and consider the implications of this for a moment. How many times have we come upon people with the requisite technical skills but they were people that we or others just couldn't work with? When you reflect upon teams gone wrong, is it because the members could not do the actual task itself? That is far less often the case. Recruiting teams are trained to ensure the right background, education, experiences, and performance. No, more often it is that people do what they do differently, with different assumptions about what is right and how people should treat each other, and they cannot work together as an outcome of the resulting unresolved conflict. Not so sure about that? Well consider the indisputable fact that companies spend enormous sums of money just trying to get people to get along. I know, they have spent a good chunk of it on my services over the span of my career.

We have coaches and we have training programs. We take assessments to learn about ourselves and others. We have had all the "one to one" meetings we can probably stomach, and we have been involved in conflict resolution individually, in pairs, and in groups. We have received and given performance evaluations on how well we work with others. Face it, we have created a massive industry to respond to the marks we get and give on "plays well with others," which we first started dealing with in grade school. Again, I probably shouldn't mock, I have done very well in my career helping people with these problems and running or delivering many of the interventions mentioned above. But how do we get there in the first place? To paraphrase Rodney King during the Los Angeles riots, "Why can't we all just get along?"[1]

The problem with scientific management in a digital age

How did we end up in this place where smart people are not able to work together? To answer that question, we need look no further than the place where we first got started at modern-day organizing and at the grandfather of management science, Frederick Taylor. Taylor, the man who created "scientific management", focused on the role of the employee as the fulcrum of a new way of working. He believed that the selection, training, and development of each employee was critical and that you could not leave it to employees to train themselves and have the kind of efficiency needed by, what were then becoming, modern organizations. While there was a fair bit of presenting his evidence in the best possible light, overlooking those things that did not support his theories, there is little doubt that his methods did add greatly to organization efficiency and the increase in affluence of both the company and the worker. We can debate further about who, in the end, benefited more from his theories.

Taylor's work began in earnest in the late 1800s. What is truly startling is the hold that his work and thinking still has on some organizational leaders today. I have worked with people of great intelligence and world-class educational backgrounds who still adhere to the Taylor-like belief that if you break down a job into its core tasks, and then enforce compliance with those tasks, you will consistently achieve measurable success. I'm not talking about moving pig iron, I'm talking about much more sophisticated and non-manual work. These leaders clearly still support the idea of moving control for work from the worker to management. They see management's job as the planning of work and the employee's job as executing work—pure Taylorism.

What I find most interesting about this is that these leaders apply Taylorism to knowledge work. I'm not so sure even Taylor would have done this, had knowledge work existed in his time. My favorite Taylor quote is this:

> One of the very first requirements for a man who is fit to handle
> pig iron as a regular occupation is that he shall be so stupid and so
> phlegmatic that he more nearly resembles in his mental make-up the

> ox than any other type. The man who is mentally alert and intelligent is for this very reason entirely unsuited to what would, for him, be the grinding monotony of work of this character.[2]

I am guessing that Taylor might have been thinking that the "man who is mentally alert and intelligent" was more fit for management than labor. But, in a world where entry-level workers are now much more educated than in 1890 and where we recognize that most people are more "mentally alert and intelligent" than Taylor was perhaps giving the common man credit for in the late 1800s, this description might apply to the whole employee population. In the current time our Taylor-minded leaders have missed how the advances in education have changed the playing field for Taylor-like theories. This applies to labor as well as knowledge work and even more so to the new reality of relationship work, which we discussed earlier.

In our modern world the advances in education, technology, and change have rendered Taylorism completely anachronistic. But consider all the times you have seen clearly demonstrated from a manager or leader that they absolutely believe that: 1) they know more than those they manage; and 2) their task is to get those they manage to act, not think. Usually this is phrased as "executing" those things that are "best practices" but the reality is that the 10 cent words used are the silk purse made from the sow's ear of "do what I say, because I know better than you."

This fundamental belief has spawned another whole industry of identifying those "best practices" and then creating the business processes and practices and the roles that carry out those practices. Do we ever go to the market to hire without a role description? Very rarely. We hire consultants and develop (or buy) competency models and create a morass of job descriptions full of detail that we use, somewhat, maybe, in our hiring processes and then almost never look at again. We take those competency models and use them in our performance management practices or talent development processes. And doesn't that just feel good all round? When we meet with our manager to look at the sum and substance of what we do, filtered through the reductionist lens of a performance management document or system of record, don't we then truly feel the expansive possibilities and the belief in us as human beings to learn, change, and be fulfilled? Am I being sarcastic, again?

Mind you, I have built and deployed role descriptions, hiring processes, competency models, and all the rest. And I have done so multiple times. Does this make me a huge hypocrite? I didn't think so at the time. I took my own scientific and logic-based thinking processes that I was taught and tried to create something that was fair, data driven, and valuable. Since I was hired to create simple, manageable answers I did so. It didn't occur to me at the time that the request was what was wrong, and people were just too complicated and nuanced for these tools and systems. But, in the end, I found that these models, while not evil or fully wrong in and of themselves, were also not enough. They fell far short of describing the person sitting in front of their manager. If they were used as the last word and authoritative tool that quantified people, they fell woefully short. If they were used as a place to start and guide honest dialogue, they could actually be very helpful. But, again, it was when they became a formula that drove opportunity and wealth that they became corrupted and divisive instead of useful. There is a whole book that could be written on the quantified human being and what this has done to us, our organizations, and our society. In fact, a friend of mine is probably going to write it and, if I have my way, I'll help her. But for now, I just ask you to accept, on face value and your own experience, that how we measure each other has real problems. And, if there are problems with this, what do we do?

Why personizing matters more

I have a hard time thinking of any thought leader who has been actively and consistently enriching our understanding of people in organizations more than Ed Schein. His work is as relevant today as it was in the 1960s, arguably even more so. While his work on group dynamics, career anchors, process consultation, and culture are all groundbreaking, it is his current work where he emphasizes the role of interpersonal relationships that I am currently most inspired by. His premise is simple, yet powerful. He distinguishes between several levels of relationships and shows us that the key to effective organizations lies not in the way roles are defined and organized but in how we understand each other as whole human beings. He points out something that we have forgotten or overlooked, especially those of us in the HR field. And it is this—roles are nearly always dehumanizing.

That's a fairly tough statement, especially if part of what you contribute to in an organization is built on role profiles and descriptions and all that those impact, such as hiring, evaluating, terminating, developing, etc. But it may be the tough love that HR leaders and teams need to receive to shake us out of our reverie and our unchallenged belief that some of our very common practices are badly broken and causing us more harm than good.

You may be thinking that this view is too pessimistic. After all, don't job descriptions and role profiles and their related models and systems make it easier to understand how to achieve, get promoted, and be more successful? Yes, they absolutely do. We can use these systems to show that we are ready for the next role and that we are a valuable asset to the system. Let me repeat that: a valuable asset *to the system*. Therein lies the subtle but real danger. We have now confined and defined success in a way that is inflexible and, furthermore, becomes a self-fulfilling prophecy. No matter what we try, we will always be subject to the systems we create becoming simplified. This seems good when we do it since the simplification makes things more subjective, takes out bias, and is infinitely easier than taking the time to train people to evaluate each individual against themselves instead of against each other. Individualized reviews of performance don't help us distribute rewards and opportunities at scale. (Or easily limit and contain the spend.)

Those descriptions and models make it easier to be successful, but they throttle the definition of what success is and do not allow for it to evolve organically or at pace. That is the danger we often overlook. We can now only be as good as the system and often the system is no longer good enough.

I'll sum up the danger with a remark made to me by a very success-ful CFO of a major company. We were talking about the way we had calculated and averaged performance and how it ended up being so simplified that it really did not represent the truth in many specific situations but that, overall, it was right in the aggregate across the company. I demurred and said that this approach resulted in some unfair outcomes for some. His response was that, yes, it was wrong, but it was useful and worked overall for the purposes of managing to the budget. He would rather it be wrong, but easy to use, than right and much more difficult and complicated to administer. He was not a cynic either, he was a good guy. He just could not see how to get it right and make it easy to implement, and so that was the price we paid. At this point I truly felt that those of us in HR had let him down by not finding a different way.

The Scheins' levels of relationships

The Scheins talk about four different levels of relationships. Interestingly, there is no level zero. They go from Level −1 to Level 1, Level 2, and Level 3. Level −1 is what they simply refers to as total impersonal domination and coercion. It is a relationship, just a very negative one where we don't treat each other as humans at all. This is something we see less and less in organizations, but we also know that there are organizations that exist out of the more accepted realm of law and morals.

There is no level zero because that means there is really just no relationship at all. Level 1, the Scheins describe as transactional role and rule-based supervision, service, and most forms of "professional" helping relationships. Does that sound familiar? Are you surprised that this description, which probably fits most of the organizations you have encountered, is only Level 1? I was. But as I learned more, I realized that it made sense. The Scheins describe Level 2 relationships as personal, cooperative, trusting relationships as in friendships and effective teams. Finally, Level 3 are emotionally intimate total mutual commitments. The Scheins say that the degree of personization is the critical differentiator between levels. They define personization as follows:

> Personization is the process of mutually building a working relationship with a fellow employee, teammate, boss, subordinate, or colleague based on trying to see that person as a whole, not just in the role that he or she may occupy at the moment.[3]

They go on to say this:

> Personization has nothing to do with being nice, giving employees good jobs and working conditions, generous benefits, or flexible working hours. It has everything to do with building relationships that get the job done and that avoid the indifference, manipulation, or, worse, lying and concealing that so often arise in work relationships.[4]

Most of our working lives are spent in Level 1 relationships. Level 1 relationships are all about roles. We are assigned, or take on, a role and there is a set of expectations that go along with that role. There is also a set of expectations that goes along with identifying with a role or being seen or seeing others as their role. If I asked you to define "acting professional" you might struggle to define it, or the definitions that many of you come up with might not all align, but we all have a sense of what acting professionally looks like and feels like. We expect people to meet a set of expectations based on the role they are in, regardless of the person in the role. We expect our server in a restaurant to be helpful and put our needs first. We expect a doctor to maybe ask questions another person would not. We usually answer each other's questions and try to respond to statements and positions as if they had some merit, at least initially. We "behave professionally" even though there is often an undercurrent of emotion that does not align with that behavior. That is what is expected of us in our roles.

In many ways our roles, be it CEO or entry-level worker, are almost caricatures. There are unwritten rules that we live by and, more to the point, that we don't often acknowledge or challenge, we just accept them. We look askance at those who don't accept the unspoken code. Those who break the rules cause real disruption that nearly always reflects back on them and their suitability for their role, in our eyes. Not sure about that? Think back to the last time you saw someone get screaming mad or break down in tears in a work situation. Did you consider it normal or was there a feeling that what was happening was "wrong"? In these situations, we often see that person as weak, out of control, or deserving of shame or recrimination, even if we don't say it in the meeting or even ever say it out loud. We know that the rules of professionalism have been broached and it makes us uncomfortable. As a result, most of us learn to play our roles and mask or stifle those feelings that make us most human.

But hey, what's wrong with that? We can't work effectively if everyone is crying and laughing and yelling at each other, can we? I'm not advocating that all work meetings become dysfunctional family holiday dinners. But what I am saying is that there is a limit to what we can do if we just adhere to our roles. This might have not always been the case or, at least, it may have been less obviously a problem, but the world has changed. In a world where the problems we are trying to solve change so quickly, and where the nature of the problems has become more complex, we don't have the time to rewrite and adjust our roles to meet the needs of our current context. We need to be able to make changes in real time and together. This means that we have to step out of the role we are in and be able to judge its usefulness and change it at will. We can't do that when we *are the role*, we can only do that as human beings who play roles as needed but are not defined by them.

This brings us to Level 2, which is marked by treating each other as whole human beings. When we get to know each other as people we learn about what each other likes and dislikes, thinks they are good at and aspires to be better at, what they value, what their situation is (home and family, living, commuting, etc.), and what they hope to get out of or achieve in life. A whole person is so much more than a role person. And it leads to some things that do not necessarily happen at the Level 1 role-based relationship. If we know someone as a whole person, we are more likely to make and honor commitments and promises to each other. We agree to support or, at least, not undermine each other in what we have agreed to do together. We are less likely to lie to each other or withhold information needed to get our work done.

Think of a time when you worked with someone whom you truly knew as a whole person (and I am desperately hoping you have had that experience). Remember how that person "had your back" and was someone you counted on to be honest with you, even if painfully so. Think on the things you got accomplished together and how you counted on each other for support and for their commitment to the work, even if it became incredibly demeaning at times. Recall the feeling of warm camaraderie when you succeeded and celebrated that success. And think about how, even though the work itself may have been hard, it felt easier because of who you were working with.

Contrast that with a time where you knew that you were just filling a role and seen as totally fungible with another person playing that same role. Maybe you were even told that. "I can replace you tomorrow! There are plenty of people out there who would kill to be in your position." Think about the information people didn't share. Recall those who undermined you because it really wasn't about you, it was just business. Did it feel like "just business"? Did those words ring hollow and now seem more like a cloak of excuse and rationale for unkind or selfish behavior?

I don't know what your personal experiences have been, but I have certainly experienced both of these types of relationships, alongside many others with whom I have talked over the years. But maybe the negative examples I just gave above are not actually the villain in Level 1 relationships. Maybe it is the normative and banal role-based relationships that really cause us difficulties in a fast-moving digital world with change all around us. Because it is sticking to our "swim lanes" that often is one of the biggest barriers to transformation in an organization. We have been organized into our respective roles and, most often, those roles are set up to execute the plans and strategies of others. As those plans and strategies age faster and faster, we still are waiting around for those others in management roles to update, reorganize, and recast our roles. That's their job. Our job is to fulfill the role. Often, we know that the role itself, and what is being asked of it (and us), has passed its expiry date. But, somewhere along the spectrum of indifference and fear of challenging the boss, we remain in the role, doing things we know are no longer optimal or valuable, because we don't feel safe or allowed to do otherwise.

Contrast that with a world where we can say, "Is this what we really should be doing? What do we need to change to do this better? Based on what I know about you, is this really the best role for you to play right now? Is this the best work for me?" What if we can have that discussion openly, without worrying that someone might say that the role we now think we should play doesn't exist (there's no sanctioned role profile) and so there might not be a place for us? Sound farfetched? Have you ever tried to create a new role in an organization that was clearly needed but that didn't fit the structure, banding system, groupings, etc.? The larger organizations get the more difficult it is to create new roles. The trust that we can do something different without it being controlled so we don't take advantage, or so we can ensure equitable treatment, is nearly always missing. We play it safe and we limit our world to a documented and (now) inadequate structure that we put in place, but which now seems to be just too much work to dismantle or deviate from. We don't feel safe enough and we don't trust each other enough when we are just roles to each other, we only do that when we see each other as whole humans.

One question then becomes, which level is best? Let's define best as delivering the best outcomes and results and making the people who work there the happiest and most fulfilled. I think you see that, in my view (and the Scheins' view) Level 2 is a clear winner over Level 1, especially in our digital world. But how about Level 3—emotionally intimate total mutual commitments? When I talk to leadership teams about the value of these levels of relationships and what makes organizations thrive, this is the one that gets the immediate "Well, we know it's not Level 3!" This is usually accompanied by some nervous laughter and a glance at the senior most HR person in the room to show them that they understand boundaries in the workplace. Intimacy has no place in the workplace, that's just asking for trouble. Well... maybe we should look closer at what the term intimacy means, as well as the rest of the terms the Scheins use, before we just move forward with our assumptions.

While the word intimacy often has connotations of a sexual nature, the word itself can also denote "close familiarity or friendship." The Gallup organization has a well-known, and well-researched, employee engagement survey that thousands of companies around the globe use. It consists of only 12 questions. The Q12, as they refer to it, has been pared down to the essence. Only the questions that truly correlate to high levels of engagement *and* business outcomes are used. In my conversations with Gallup research scientists, I was told that one of these 12 questions was both the most controversial and also absolutely critical—a highly accurate bellwether for employee engagement. The question? "I have a best friend at work." I was told that this is the question that gets challenged the most. People are frustrated that it is not clear. "Does my best friend work with me, you mean?" or "Do I have a best work friend, is that it?" They also said that they had tried hundreds of combinations of the question but the reason they stick with the statement "I have a best friend at work" (of which people can note their degree of agreement or disagreement on a Likert-type scale) is because that particular phrasing, despite the questions and complaints, is what works. No other version correlated as highly with engagement and demonstrable business success and outcomes.

I love this story because it actually highlights part of what our "professional," or normative, Level 1 relationships at work have done to us. Role-based relationships remove intimacy. I cannot have a close familiarity or friendship with someone whom I treat as a fungible resource who just has to complete their duties. But we have become so accepting of the "professional" workplace, and the dangers of getting closer to people, that we get confused and frustrated by the phrase "best friend" when it comes to who we work with. I do understand that intimate relationships that are also sexual can cause real difficulties and violate the law and, even more importantly, disadvantage and exploit people. But are those dysfunctional relationships really about intimacy or are they about power? I worked for someone I have great respect for who fell in love with someone on their team. What did they do? They made the necessary changes to no longer have a reporting relationship and they remain happily married to this day. I also know of couples who have started businesses together and who are very effective business partners. I would argue that a loving, sexual relationship is different from some of those that start in the workplace where it is more about power or entitlement. I guess someone else will have to write that book.

Moving beyond sexual intimacy at work, let's look at emotionally intimate total mutual commitments. Notice that the Scheins start with "intimate" being modified with "emotionally." This means there is feeling but it can be the strong feelings we have for friends instead of lovers. Then there is "total mutual commitment." Wow! That's powerful! If you talk to some of the founders of highly successful startups I think, upon reflection, that they would say that total mutual commitment does a very good job of describing what they had with a small team of good friends who gave their all during long days and nights to achieve a shared vision. That is what emotionally intimate total mutual commitment looks like at work. You might have been part of a team in a larger organization that had that kind of camaraderie and commitment as well. I know I have, and it felt amazing. The work product was quite amazing too.

The only thing I actually worry about with Level 3 relationships at work is that they are hard to have at scale. I received a call from one of my favorite clients during the early days of the Black Lives Matter protests in 2020. They were distressed. They said to me, "Michael, I have 10,000 employees in my care, over half of whom are Black or are people of color, and I have no idea what their experience is truly like here [at the company] and what I can do to truly make sure it is one of dignity, respect, and equity. I don't know them all and don't know how to have that conversation with thousands of people in a meaningful way!" Let's face it, it's hard to have 10,000 best friends at work. We have a limited capacity for intimate friendships because of the time and effort they take. Now, I don't think we have to abandon Level 3 relationships at work, we just need to realize that they will happen on a smaller scale, at least in larger organizations, and that they probably cannot exist within a setting of Level 1 relationships. They need a garden of Level 2 relationships to grow in. If you have ever had the joy of working in a place like that, you will know what I mean. If you haven't, then it might be time to start moving your organization in that direction. Let's talk about how to do just that.

Get engaged with goals before roles

One way to activate Humanizing Before Organizing is to consider the power of goals before roles. We have discussed the value of North Stars and clear missions or visions in getting people to come together and make congruent decisions, even when they are not together, but now it is time to look at how to leverage these things to get the work done.

When you focus on goals before roles, you set up a space where you can organize and reorganize in the best way to get the job done. In my consulting practice I refer to this as "designing work." Designing work, as a driver of Humanizing Before Organizing, is knowing how to organize with the people we work with to achieve our goals, with little concern for power and status. The fundamental question of designing work is, "Do we know how to organize ourselves to get stuff done?" Learning how to organize ourselves is not too difficult, it is another thing to deal with the issues of power and status baked into our modern organizations.

While there are many ways to look at organizing work, I like to start with the foundational model of organization design and then work inwards. I have had the great privilege of working closely with Dr Sue Mohrman from USC's Center for Effective Organizations. I have been a student of Sue's writing, theory, and research for over 25 years. I have her textbooks still on my shelf from my graduate school days in the mid-1990s. In the recent few years before the publication of the book you are reading, I got introduced to Sue personally and we developed a friendship and working relationship. When she was working on the organization (re)design of one of the big, global consumer packaged goods companies, she called me in to support their implementation and change efforts that would be needed for the design to be successfully implemented.

Sue is now, arguably, the leading mind in organization design in the world. With her former colleague, the now deceased Jay Galbraith, Sue has worked with countless organizations to understand and use the Star Model that Jay is known for. Sue's research continues to this day to influence how companies go about using the Star Model to do organization design. But the approach goes beyond design. Sue's colleague (and my graduate thesis advisor and mentor) Dr Chris Worley, of USC and Pepperdine University, has spoken of "design as change." What does this mean? First, a quick look at the Star Model. There are some different variations of the model but Figure 9.1 shown here is one I have used with Sue and colleagues in the field.

At its simplest, the Star Model says that all of the elements shown in this picture need to be addressed to effectively design an organization and that they are all interrelated and dependent on the others. This is a systems view of organizations; you cannot effectively address one of them unless you address them all and changes in one impact the others. Don't worry, we are not going to dig deep into organization design theory, there are plenty of resources out there for that if you want to do that. What I am going to focus on here is the simple idea of the system and what thinking in a systems mindset causes us to do. It causes us to ask questions when, or if, something is being changed.

As an example, if you change an organization's structure, you will need to make sure you have the right people, incentivized in the right way, with the right work processes and capabilities to do the job of the new structure, and the communication and decision-making management processes to accommodate the information flow in the new structure. You cannot just change the structure in isolation and expect all goodness to follow. Yet often we make structural changes and then the only other changes we make are to pay a manager or two more and/or let go of a few people who no longer have a chair when the music stops. But we don't necessarily spend the time to ask the questions about capabilities, work processes, management processes, etc. This can easily, and often will, lead to organizations giving lip service to the new structure or model, but not actually changing how most work gets done. Or it can lead to disillusion with leadership and disengagement or disconnection from the strategic goals, causing cynicism and lowering productivity. Again, think of companies you have been a part of that have done a reorganization of some sort. Remember all the questions people had? All the "whys" and "hows" and "whos," etc.

FIGURE 9.1   THE STAR MODEL

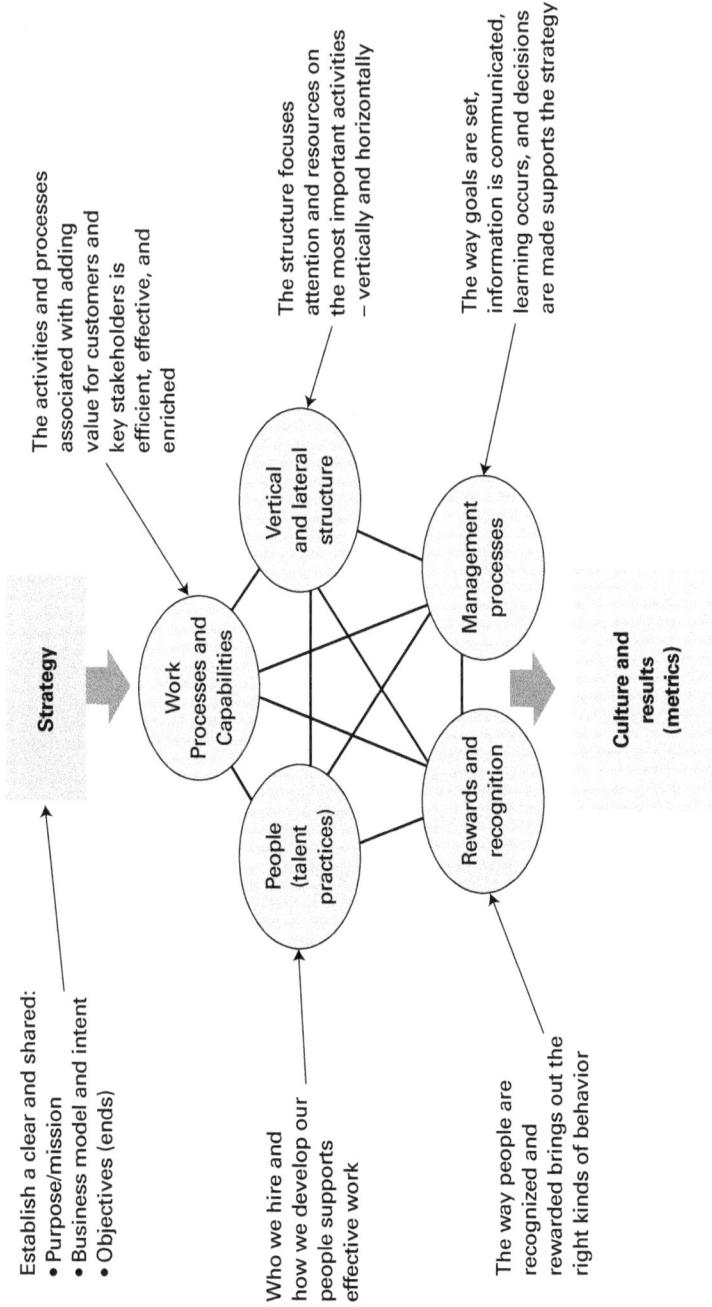

Establish a clear and shared:
• Purpose/mission
• Business model and intent
• Objectives (ends)

Strategy

Work Processes and Capabilities

The activities and processes associated with adding value for customers and key stakeholders is efficient, effective, and enriched

Vertical and lateral structure

The structure focuses attention and resources on the most important activities – vertically and horizontally

Management processes

The way goals are set, information is communicated, learning occurs, and decisions are made supports the strategy

People (talent practices)

Who we hire and how we develop our people supports effective work

Rewards and recognition

The way people are recognized and rewarded brings out the right kinds of behavior

Culture and results (metrics)

SOURCE Adapted from Galbraith (2014)[5]

Most often when people think of "organization design" they just think of structure and sort of leave the rest alone. Maybe they consider rewards and people, but usually it is only the rewards of the people who win or lose power or status in the reorganization. Heck, I've seen huge reorganizations done for the core purpose of just getting rid of one executive, as an excuse to allow them to save face. I suppose that many senior leaders do that knowing that their time on the chopping block may come and they want to be treated with the same deference and allowed to talk to the next headhunter with a solid story for why they left the company, allowing them to get another job at similar rank and status.

When Chris Worley talks about "design as change," I think he means the process of examining all the other systemic changes that might be needed to make the system work (using the Star Model as the system) and identifying the resultant changes required to make it all work. As an example, part of the organization design implementation work with the large CPG firm I mentioned was getting people throughout the organization to understand the Star Model and simply say, "Okay, if we make this change (whatever change is being discussed, large or small, global or local) what has to happen in the other elements of the Star Model to make that change work and stick?" That in itself is what design as change looks like.

If we then go back to the value of goals before roles, we see that achieving goals might require us to change how we organize to do our work—and it is hard to do that unless we know the people we work with as whole human beings. As mentioned, there are often structural things in the way of doing just that.

I said earlier that I believe HR as a function in companies is at a crossroads. The transactional work being done will continue to be quickly siphoned off to be completed by AI, bots, and other forms of smart technology that can do those jobs better and faster. So, if HR does not want to fade into being merely a technology vendor management office, they will have to look at the new places value is created in a digital world—in getting people together who can work with each other. That means providing them with the tools and impetus to get to personize. It means working to minimize policy and regulation and providing just-in-time support on those things that must remain. It means being a role model of understanding design as change. It means a lot more Human in Human Resources.

For us as individuals and leaders, it starts (as always) with our changing behaviors by asking, in this case, the questions that create humanization in an organization.

The five questions of Humanizing Before Organizing

These questions are aimed at getting to know each other as whole human beings, but also at doing this in a work setting. There are certainly other things we do to get to know each other such as talk about home, family, interests, etc. We also can leave the work setting and spend time together socially over a lunch, drinks, dinner, etc. During times when we are prevented from being together in person, such as in the COVID-19 pandemic during which some of this book was written, we can also schedule time where we promise not to talk about work but to get to know each other better. We can even do this in facilitated ways—and many of my client organizations have seen the value in this. But, regardless of how we are connecting, we can use these questions to better know and understand each other.

Question 1: When are you at your best?

Question 2: How will we know when things have started to go sideways?

Question 3: How could we work better together next time?

Question 4: What really matters to you?

Question 5: What do you want from me?

---

1. When are you at your best?

This is the **appreciative-inquiry question**. It allows you to understand how others see themselves and what conditions help produce their best selves. I often will follow this question with asking someone to tell me of a time that they were at their best—what happened, what factors contributed to them showing up as their best selves, what have they learned from times like these, is there a pattern? (Full credit to Michael Bungay Stanier and his book *Do More Great Work* for the Great Work Stories exercise that inspires this question.) This is a question that needs more than a one-word or one-line answer. All of the questions here are catalysts for conversation and exploration as you get to know someone as a whole person.

2. How will we know when things have started to go sideways?

This is the **permission-to-not-be-perfect question**. Just acknowledging that things can go sideways is a huge help in relationships as it gives you permission to deal with it when it happens. It is a funny phenomenon, but when relationships start to go a little sideways the thing we mostly feel, whether we are fully cognizant of it or not, is shame. We are ashamed that it is not working well because it was before and now there is a problem. That shame often turns to irritation or even fear, depending on the nature of the relationship. Having permission to talk about when things go sideways opens the door to addressing it and mitigates the shame and the feelings it causes. This question also gives you tools to recognize when things are not going as well as they should. If you know, and have told others, that you tend to withdraw when things go sideways then others can ask, "Did something go sideways here?" when they see you withdraw.

3. How could we work better together next time?

This is the **continuous-improvement question**. It allows us to modify the social contract of how we work together. It is useful for one-on-one dialogue and exploration of how we work with each other and allows us to create a social contract and state clear expectations of each other. It is also valuable for more than just two people talking. I am amazed at how often people meet without ever talking about the meeting itself. Not the subject being discussed, but the effectiveness of the meeting. I'd say it is because most meetings are just rocking examples of effective use of time and clear decisions made, but you might choke and spit up on this nice book. We all know that the majority of meetings are, at best, bland and not particularly useful. I don't even need to describe them at their worst.

4. What really matters to you?

This is the **"But who are you really?" question,** which starts to get closer to the core of what motivates and drives others. It doesn't mean that you will share all of those things, but it gives you the opportunity to understand them and respect them. I had a colleague once, Jim, who was a very different person than me. One of us drank alcohol, the other didn't. One was Republican, the other Democrat, and our choice mattered to us. One of us had values based in their Christian faith, the other was no longer a believer in religion; one of us was ex-military and supported access to guns, one of us was a proponent of gun control. I could go on. But Jim and I got to know each other as whole human beings and I can tell you that he became a good friend and someone I thoroughly enjoyed working with. Even though I knew we had some fundamental differences in how we looked at the world, we both respected what mattered to each other. Discussions of faith, politics, etc. did not have to factor into our work and good wine bars also carry club soda. But knowing that Jim deeply cared about his family, was honest and upfront, and really cared about helping others be more and do more brought us together in a way that we never would have had we remained caricatures or categories to each other. We knew what really mattered to each of us, and those things we shared brought us closer and we respected the differences.

5. What do you want from me?

This is the **bottom-line question.** I saved this one for last as it is absolutely foundational to human relationships. I want you to say this question out loud. When you do, I want you to ask it two ways. The first is in that way that is irritated and clearly says the other person is an intrusion or unwelcome. Now, we don't often use the phrase that way with others, at least not to their face, but we say it about them to ourselves or sometimes others who we think might share our view of that person. "What do you want?" often sounds so negative when actually muttered that we forget what it sounds like when asked from a place of love or generosity. A truly curious and willing "What do you want from me?" gives people permission to actually ask for what they want. I encourage you to ask this question from a place of true caring and interest and watch how it changes relationships in a powerful way or makes clear what you can do to make an impact. This book is my way of answering the question for those of you who picked it up. I truly hope it is useful to your work and life.

Endnotes

1 thetruthisviral (2010) Can We All Just Get Along? For The Kids & Old People? RODNEY KING SPEAKS! *YouTube* [online] https://www.youtube.com/watch?v=1sONfxPCTU0 (archived at https://perma.cc/3XV2-J8VL)

2 Taylor, F W (2009) [1911] *Principles of Scientific Management*, Cornell University Library, New York

3 Schein, E H and Schein, P (2018) *Humble Leadership: The power of relationships, openness, and trust*, Berrett-Koehler Publishers, Oakland CA

4 Ibid

5 Galbraith, J R (2014) *Designing Organizations: Strategy, structure, and process at the business unit and enterprise levels*, Jossey-Bass & Pfeiffer Imprints, Wiley, San Francisco CA

10

Your Heart of Transformation— Making It Strong

Getting going building your heart of transformation

You've made it this far. We have talked about why our world of work needs the six capabilities that lie at *The Heart of Transformation*. We have seen that the old capabilities have not been eliminated, they have just ceased to do what they need to do by themselves. They now must be embraced and enfolded by the new capabilities that come before them and ensure that they are still valid and useful. We have heard from people who have been at the forefront of building the six capabilities and we've seen how this has resulted in the outcomes that we are looking for in a world of complex problems, continuous change, and digital demands. Finally, we have come to understand some of the things that allow change to happen or make it easier such as knowing why we want to change and being purpose-driven, keeping change simple, and realizing that change is individual and not a systemic or organizational problem to be solved by others. We now know that true change, driven by a strong heart of transformation, is something that we are responsible for in ourselves—each of us. It is our collective personal changes that can add up to an organization transforming. There is no shortcut, there is no other way.

Given all that, I have, hopefully, convinced you of your role in building your heart of transformation and changing your organization for good. That makes it time for the final part of this book, which is helping you take the concepts from it and make them your day-to-day reality, not just a good idea unimplemented and not just a "one and done" lesson that is taken in but doesn't stick or cause actual change to happen. As you may have guessed, there is work yet to be done. But, not to worry, in this last section we will cover what you need to do. We will answer the question, "What do I have to do and who do I have to be to embrace these ideas, learn about myself, and ultimately behave in a new way?" We will help you to:

- Get started. And get started again. And yet again.

- Choose your priorities and not try to boil the ocean or get overwhelmed by change—finding the right things to focus on in the right time and in a way that you can do it without superhuman effort.

- Make your plan and draw your roadmap—pathfinding for your transformation journey.

- Disrupt your habits and recognize the patterns that keep you in the old capabilities or in the less useful behaviors you have become accustomed to.

- Turn your personal debrief insights into learning by remembering to interrogate yourself and see the patterns in what you discover.

- Create new patterns and habits to try on that reflect the way the behaviors in this book will work for you.

- Make clear the value of preserving your thinking time and getting you engaged in asking for the help you will need to do that. And, make no mistake, while this is a personal journey, there is no need to make it alone. In fact, that is just the thing you don't want to do!

- Create your advisory board of people who see you as you are and tell you what you can't yet see about yourself easily when looking at yourself through your eyes.

- Identify the tools and resources you will need to do all of the above more easily and simply—some of which are in this book, some of which you will be able to download (for free, of course), and some of which you will find waiting for you out there in all sorts of unexpected places.

We will do all of this in a way that is much easier than you might expect having just read that list. Remember that word I cherish so much? It's "useful." In order to make this book useful I have already distilled down the capabilities of a heart of transformation into some very simple, if powerful, questions. I will make sure that the rest of the guidance for how to effectively integrate asking these questions into your life is just as straightforward, achievable, and useful. This section is about achieving heart health—developing a strong and vibrant heart of transformation that ensures you run the race at pace, full of energy and hope, and with your eyes firmly on the amazing road ahead of you.

Begin the begin—how do you start building a heart of transformation?

This book was both incredibly difficult and surprisingly easy to write. Actually, that's not true. A more accurate way of saying it would be to say that this book was incredibly difficult *not to write* and surprisingly easy to write. As I type this on my Mac, it is the day, scheduled months and months ago, that this last chapter draft is due to my editor. When the final manuscript is completed it will be just over a year that I began this journey and about 10 months of writing. Now, here's my confession—I did not spend the entire 10 months writing the book. Okay, you knew that already. I also worked a lot, changed jobs, then started a new business, spent time with my family and friends, found time to run, hike, bike, swim, etc. But I was writing all along, sometimes meeting my scheduled deadlines, but not always. During that time, we also had a global pandemic arrive accompanied by an incredibly contentious political environment in the United

States, along with the related social unrest, which had impacts across the globe—2020 was an eventful year for many of us, to say the least.

Recognizing all that was happening around me I realized I needed to get smart and block out time on my calendar to write. I had it all set up, I had a special color in my calendar for the writing days (and the word "Book!" looking up at me plaintively from the screen), and a set of very reasonable deadlines from the amazing team at Kogan Page. Deadlines I initially said I thought we could probably push up as I could just not conceive that I needed that much time to write the book. I was wrong.

I had the best of intentions, I had a plan, and I was ready to go. Here's where I want to get back to why the book was incredibly difficult *not to write* and surprisingly easy *to write*. I have to, somewhat shamefacedly, admit that I probably spent more time not writing the book during those blocked times than writing the book. Why was that and what did I do with the time you ask? Good question. I spent the non-writing writing time doing several highly unproductive things. Chief among them was worrying about not writing when I should be writing. Second was worrying that when I tried to write, nothing intelligent would come out of my head. Third, but probably most damning, was avoiding writing because I could not see the whole book in my mind—the end was not in sight. The chapter that needed writing was only the title I had created in an outline months earlier and, when I looked at it, I thought, "How in the world is there a whole chapter worth reading in that heading? What was I thinking? I'm doomed!"

Well, obviously, I was not doomed as you have this book in your hands or on your e-reader or audio book and, if you've got this far, then it must have been worth the reading. What happened? What was the turning point that transformed me into a writing machine? How did I flip the switch that changed everything? I didn't.

But what I did do was look at my fear and frustration—my doubts and feeling of being stuck—and despaired. But then I paused, took a breath, and looked at a time when I *had* successfully written something and asked myself, "Well, how did I actually do that?" And the answer was quite simple. Shockingly simple—I started.

What I learned about myself is that my doubts and insecurities were illusory, but they were an incredibly effective tool for keeping me from just starting. I couldn't see the end of the road, so I hesitated to take the first step. But, when I finally forced myself to start to write, the words came. I would literally sit down, look at my computer screen, and see the great blankness staring back at me, then I'd choke down all the worries that nothing useful would come and just start writing. Once I started, I flew, and suddenly I'd stop and flex my tired fingers, stand up and stretch, and then look down at 3,000, 4,000, even 5,000 words I'd written and wonder how they had got there, but be delighted that they had. As I continued to write, this truth about myself—that if I just started then I would find a path—began to take hold. I still had moments of fighting with the anxiety, but I began to get better at winning the fight.

You see, I was struggling because I believed I could write a 75,000-word book—and I couldn't. But that wasn't the task. I didn't have to have a book done that day. All I needed was to write part of the next chapter. But even when that seemed overwhelming and I couldn't do it I realized there was one thing that I could do—I could start. And I could start again once I'd got a few thousand words done, or a previous chapter submitted for review. This journey was not a long continuous trek, it was a series of starts. Over and over, I just had to start.

There was a corny movie in the 1980s that has a line that has always stayed in my head. The main character, who has all sorts of relational problems, is talking to his therapist and trying to figure out how he is ever going to make the changes he wants in his rapidly deteriorating life. The therapist looks at him and says, "If an alcoholic wants me to cure him you know what I say? First, stop drinking." It's strange how a line from a silly movie, which I don't know if I've seen again since, has taken up residence in my psyche. But the psychiatrist's advice is a profound truth. If you want to do something that seems overwhelming or impossible, the only thing you can do is start doing it.

That is my wish for you with this book. You now have the six capabilities that lie at the heart of transformation and the questions that activate each capability—and now you know how to use them, so you just start using them. Don't worry about how it will turn out. Ignore the fear that they will just make you sound like you don't know everything or are a work in progress (you don't, and you are, and so is everyone else, so just ask them). In the next several sections I am going to give you more tools and support for your new life as a transformational leader or person; think of them as the support network the recovering alcoholic has. You will find advice from others on what they do to be successful, you will learn how to build a community of supporters around you, you will be given maxims you can cling onto when the going gets rough, you will receive the reminders of your current success, and you will use these approaches to make new friends who are on the journey right along with you. All these things I will provide to you or show you how to get. But only you can start.

Being foolish for fun and profit

One more thing about the attitude you need to get started. The great 20th-century philosopher Cher is widely quoted as having said, "Until you're ready to look foolish, you'll never have the possibility of being great." I'm not sure if she actually said it, but I think of her every time I get ready to potentially look foolish for a good reason. If you are not willing to put yourself out there, you will never get out there. If you are not willing to ask questions, you will always want for answers. If you are not willing to fall, you will never climb.

I often wear a kilt when I speak publicly (and, admittedly, just around the house too). I do it for a number of reasons. One, I'm of Scottish descent and always wanted a kilt in my clan colors. My entire life, people have struggled to pronounce my name. Lucky, Licky, Lackey, Leaky, even Lumpke are what I have heard or seen. It's pronounced leh-kee, like Becky, but with an L instead of a B. Literally wearing my name seemed like a way to claim it back and get it right. Also, various personality profiles describe me as outgoing, colorful, mischievous, rebellious, provocative, etc. So, maybe going against the grain just comes natural to me. It doesn't feel that way to me since as a child I was shy around strangers, lacking self-confidence, and desperately wanting to fit in, not stand out. But I'll let the therapists sort that one out. I think that the reason I like to wear it is because, to many people, it just looks odd or even silly; foolish, if you will, but people notice me. I am happy to look a little foolish if it both gets your attention and takes me down a peg or two in your eyes. I want your attention because I think I have a message worth sharing. I am happy to self-deprecate because if I am on a stage in front of you it elevates me, and I want to balance the terms of the engagement so we can talk, not just so you can listen. I want us to engage, not for you to merely judge. I want my foolishness to make me accessible so we can learn and grow together.

That is also the mindset that helps us start to do something new. It helps us begin what we don't know how to finish. That allows us to risk looking foolish so we can grow in our ability to help ourselves and others.

In medieval times, the Fool was the one person who could call out the truth about the monarch. They could relieve the tension of the human foibles of those who were literally taken as speaking for, and being like, God. They were able to do so because they put on the costume of the Fool and therefore it was all a joke. But a joke that reflected uncomfortable truths, as the best jokes do. Foolishness is a superpower if you will only embrace it. Once you are willing to play the fool, then no one can stop you from growing, learning, and helping others to see the truths that just may set them free. I encourage you to embrace the wisdom of starting with the faith of the foolish. Therein lies the path to greatness.

Where do you start building a heart of transformation?

This is the first choice to make. It's not nearly as hard as you might think because wherever you start is likely to be just fine. This is not a choice with huge consequences. Some places are still easier than others, however, so a good first place to start asking these questions is with someone else who is embarking on the same journey of asking them as well. Some of you reading this will have received the book as part of a program of transformational change or culture creation that I, or someone I know and work with, is facilitating in your group, unit, or organization. Or it may be a part of a small leadership learning cohort we are working on in the senior leadership of your company. In these cases, it is easy to find people to start working this way with as you will all be learning together. In other cases, you might be reading this on your own or there is no program in your company, someone just liked the idea and passed out copies of the book. Some of you may have picked it up in an airport bookstore or bought it online for whatever reason. But even if you are alone in your desire to apply these principles, approaches, and questions to your professional life, you can find people to help you. All you need to do is ask.

In the section on awkwardness in this book, I threw out one of my favorite pieces of guidance to people trying to learn, which is to "hide in plain sight." If you would like to find a safe place or person with whom to practice asking these questions (of yourself and/or of them) and then learning from that, then simply do it. Walk up to someone you know and trust and say, "Hey, I am reading this book on building a heart of transformation. In it the author recommends that I ask some specific questions and then learn from what happens in myself and others when I do. Do you have a few minutes that I can do that with you? It would really help me to see how well this works." It's that easy. You don't even have to give them a copy of the book (although you are more than welcome to do so of course!). All you have to do is walk up and ask for a little help that only requires they let you ask them a few questions, or that they ask them of you. That's it. Hiding in plain sight. Put it out there that learning and growing matters to you and they could do this small thing to help you.

Maybe you have already done that and are now ready to do this with your team or colleagues, or maybe you just want to jump straight into it without any further ado. Great, you can do that. And, if you want my advice, I would say to take it easy as you do. Don't try to do everything at once and don't worry about all the questions. Remember how I learned to swim? I just picked one thing to work on and then I just swam. Do that here. Pick one of the questions, one that intrigues you, or the one that resonates the most, or the one that you think is the most likely to be utterly useless, and then look for the opportunity to ask it. After you ask it once, download the tips and tools sheet on debriefing or flip back to the "Art of the debrief" from Chapter 5 and do the important work of extracting the initial information that will help you as you learn. If you are working with a colleague or friend, then give them a few questions from that section and ask them to debrief you. If you are both learning, then debrief each other.

I said above that I would help guide you in choosing your priorities. Here's what I want you to consider, and it may seem a bit counterintuitive, but you don't need to start where you want to drive the most change. You might be better off starting where you will extract the most learning. It's easy at this point to forget that this is about *your* change first. Driving change with others or across organizations is birthed in *your* change, especially as a leader. Start where it feels safest to try out the questions, and spend much more time on the debrief than on the initial asking of the question(s). Prioritize your learning, and increasing your comfort with asking the questions, over asking them in the "right" place. You are not going to be great at asking them at first. You are probably going to be even less effective at learning *from* them. But that will change, and you will get better every time you operationalize curiosity through the questions at the heart of transformation. That's the goal, you are your priority, don't forget that.

Your roadmap to a heart of transformation

Now I know I just said that you can really start anywhere and that might seem a bit at odds with this section talking to you about a roadmap for building a heart of transformation. But when we think of a heart of transformation there are a couple of lenses to look through:

- The Me and You Lens
- The Us and Them Lens

The first lens is the Me and You lens. Let's start with the Me part. This is the lens I am using when looking at the need for leaders to be able to change themselves before they try to lead change. We've discussed that, as a leader, I need to be able to truly understand change and empathize with the changes I am asking of those I lead by having the empathy and insight that comes with my own change struggles and journey. If I lead You, then You will be able to see my example and sense that I am not just telling you that this is *your* job, I am being open and vulnerable enough to show you this is *our* job. When You see Me embracing my own change You feel safe to do the same.

Both the Me and You are singular, but the plural, Us and Them, is important too, and that's the other lens we will use. This time we will start with Them. When I am initially contacted to help an organization with transformation, the conversation inevitably starts with the potential client telling me how they need the organization (Them) to change or that they need Them to know how to change or for Them to embrace change, etc. You get the point; they are usually starting with their Them; the organization. Rightly so, as their transformation struggle is rooted in changing the behaviors of the Them that makes up the organization. A Them that does not understand how to change and, likely, doesn't feel safe to change. Yes, getting Them to change is the outcome we need, it's just not where we start, it's where we end up, which brings us back to Us.

I have been the Me who led change in a number of organizations and circumstances in my career. I learned a lot doing that, but the learning was painful and the organizational transformation was, sadly, rarely what I hoped it would be. When approached in the past to be a "change agent" or a "positive irritant in the system" or a "provocateur towards innovation" or any other number of interesting and boldly described roles, I have taken them on with gusto, hope, and pride at being chosen as the best person to make change happen. I have both come crashing down hard and fast as well as died the slow death of a thousand cuts. Why? Because the leadership of the company tried to outsource the change to me and I, with foolish pride, accepted. I was the expert who was to make change happen, to lead change, to guide change. In other words, I was on my own and expendable and if I failed no one else really had responsibility but me. As I grew more experienced, I began to understand that I was not enough and that it took the small village of Us to lead change. And not just to believe in change and commit to change, but for the leaders around me and above me to fully inhabit the Me role described above.

Trying to lead change without a critical mass of leaders who share a vision for change and who are willing to be the individual, personal role models of change is destined to disappoint. As a group of leaders, we need to become a cohort of individuals who collaborate on the transformation we want to see. This means that we have to support one another, to trust one another, to challenge one another, to forgive one another, and to help each other see where we individually are failing and do that with the compassion that only comes with learned empathy and humility. With my clients trying to lead transformation I always start by looking at who can make up their Us and developing a plan to build relationships, trust, and a transformational Us team to lead the creation of a transformational organization of Them in achieving the ultimate goals of the change we are seeking. The lone Me is at very high risk of failure and he or she will quickly begin to burn out and lose faith. I know I have at times. I've come into situations with incredibly high hopes and big dreams and seen them shatter because I did not build up the Us I needed to share the burden. I've often wondered if that is Me as the courageous leader who is ahead of their time throwing my pearls before swine or the Me as martyr trying to force something through by will so I could shine. I'm quite sure it's both, at times, but I guess it doesn't matter. If I fail by trying to go it alone, I fail. It matters not what my own inner demons and angels are fighting for, I still let Me and Them down and nothing changes.

This brings us back to the roadmap, of which the guidelines for creating may be starting to form in your head. You start, wherever you start, and you start with you (Me). This book is written to help you to do just that. Then, you need to bring some others into the fold and become Us. That means introducing others in leadership to what you are doing to build your heart of transformation and inviting them in to do the same. If they are not interested or they think that this is your job, not theirs, then your impact will be limited. It may not be nothing, but it will be change with a small c, not Change with a capital C, and it will certainly not qualify as big-T Transformation.

I know that some of you are reading this right now and feeling that little unpleasant twinge in the pit of your stomach as you think about the other leaders around you or the leaders you are working with as their designated change agent. You don't see them getting on board and working on building a personal heart of transformation and you're hoping I'm dead wrong here. If you go forward and are able to build a transformative organization without an Us then please tell me how and I'll write a revised version of this book immediately with all credit to you. But if you come to realize that this is the sad truth, that you can't change Them without Us, then know that I feel your pain and disappointment and make sure that, next time, you really find out if it is possible and probable you will find those comrades-in-arms so you can avoid the ignominious defeat in this, a battle that you feel is truly righteous—and that you want to win with all of your heart of transformation.

However, if you have begun growing your heart of transformation and those leaders, peers, and key bosses around you have too, then you can begin to use the questions in this book to bring other individuals you work with into the fold. If We bring Them along then all goodness follows when you hit the critical mass you need, and your organization becomes one of transformation.

If you want to get those others engaged just try hiding in plain sight again. Say something like, "Hey, I'm working on building my skills as a transformational leader and one of the things I've realized is that this is not something I can do on my own. I also realize that I need to do this here, now, in the context of the change we are facing. Will you help me? In fact, will you join me? It's actually fairly straightforward, it's about asking great questions. That's it! If you'll give me a few minutes, I'll tell you more." Simple enough, no need to be sly about it.

So, that's the roadmap. You start with yourself, bring along some key others in leadership, then all of you start to bring others along one-by-one until you hit the inflection point. It's that simple and it's that difficult. Make no mistake, it is daily work and sometimes it feels slow. Sometimes you just want to do your old job and get into that comfortable spreadsheet, or design that familiar system, or run that regular meeting, or just dispense advice and approval. And that stuff can be good and valuable, for sure, but it is not transformational.

Learning from the best—aggregate and then analyze to see your patterns

In his illuminating book *The End of Average*[1] Todd Rose helps us understand how analyzing data and then aggregating the results has led to widespread assumptions that simply are not true. He shows the many ways in which we believe that "average" exists when it does not. One example he cites is taking the measurements of a specific group, in this case jet fighter pilots, and then averaging those measurements to get the size of the typical jet fighter pilot in order to design cockpits that worked well in combat conditions. When he introduced this research, I assumed that there would be a good-sized chunk of pilots who roughly fell into those average measurements. I pictured in my head a bell curve, something I've seen all my life in school, and in work, and saw all those average pilots in the rising bulge of the middle. But when the research Rose cited looked at the actual pilots, finding a single pilot out of thousands that actually hit all of the average measurements was a fool's errand. Not one of them fit all of the measurements at the average. Even when they widened the range considerably to a deviation of 90 percent from the midpoint, they only found very few. Turns out the "average" pilot did not exist in real life.

I will not summarize the whole book as I won't do it justice here. But the idea that I do want to take from Rose's writing is the one that says we are better off by not first analyzing and aggregating, but by aggregating and then analyzing. What that means, in simple terms, is looking for the patterns that emerge as you look at data and then trying to figure out what they mean and represent. In the pilot example that means they would have just looked at all the data and asked if there were any patterns that popped out. Patterns like larger finger size correlated to larger arm or leg size, or something similar. Turns out, you would not have found anything to aggregate. The disparate measurements of the pilots did not in any way represent any actual whole pilots, just a non-existent "average pilot." Unfortunately, all the cockpits of fighter jets at the time were designed to fit the average pilot and, as a result, perfectly designed to fit no one at all! This resulted in increased "pilot error" in accidents. This was eliminated by creating adjustable seating and controls in cockpits, allowing them to fit actual, individual pilots perfectly. Not average pilots who didn't exist.

Let's look at what all of this can mean to our purpose here, becoming a transformational leader or person who drives transformation in our organization. As we work on building the new patterns of our lives needed to be transformational, we have to actually start by looking at the existing patterns. The question you can ask yourself is, "What happened when things worked out well or went right?"

Recall just a few paragraphs above when I was faced with the non-writing that was keeping me from being able to write this book. I had to stop focusing on all the creative non-writing I was capable of and look just at what happened when I was actually writing. So, I sat down and said, "Okay, you have written stuff before. No, not books, but articles or papers. What happened when you successfully wrote something?" With this question in my head, I sat there trying to recall all those moments. What was I doing just before? What mood was I in? Was I alone or with others? Where was I? When did it happen? The questions were myriad, and I kept asking them and noting down some of what I found and, maybe more importantly, what I didn't find. I had some expectations, based on what I'd heard, about what helped one write. Things like going away and dedicating days or even weeks to just focused, uninterrupted writing. Having a clear schedule. Creating an outline of a chapter and then fleshing it out section by section, going back and adding more each time until the whole came together in a non-linear way, etc. But when I looked at what actually happened when I *successfully* wrote, the evidence wasn't there for those things. When I tried "writing days" I just sat there dreading the ticking of the clock as I tried to conceive of the outcome I needed at the end of the day, and I ended up doing next to nothing and feeling worse about myself into the bargain. I found that my capacity for procrastination and distraction was tremendous when I had a big chunk of time set in front of me. I did have a schedule, but I found that I did not stick to all of the times I had set aside in my calendar to meet periodic chapter goals. I tried to outline the entire chapter and found myself staring in horror at the blank page as there was no fully formed piece of literary genius springing from my mind onto the page.

What *did* I find? I began to recall those moments when I just started typing. Typing anything, just to start, and then having a moment that was almost like waking up where I looked down and saw I had written something. I also recalled those moments of realizing that I had not stuck to my micro schedule at all, but that the macro schedule (the agreement with my editorial team about when a complete first draft of a chapter was due) helped motivate me. The pattern was not the schedule. No, instead it was the agreement I had made with others. The commitment I had made to people who counted on me. That was motivation to start. And, once I started, I finished despite not knowing how I ever would when I started. I also realized that days and days of focused writing just did not work. My pattern was the need to start, see something materialize, then give my mind and fingers a break while celebrating (in a small way) the seemingly magical appearance of the words. When I did my writing in shorter bites, of no more than a few hours in any day, I was able to see progress and avoid the feeling of overwhelm. These were the patterns I saw, and these became the basis of the new habits I formed, the new plan of attack. By looking at these separate items and finding the patterns I was able to leverage that aggregation of what worked and analyze those patterns to find a path forward. It is not always easy, and I won't lie to you and tell you that I don't get sucked into old fears and patterns. But that happens a lot less than it used to and when it does it lasts much less time than it did before. All I do then is just remember or reinforce my commitment to others who count on me and then just start typing. A couple of days ago I actually wrote down the idea for my next book. While it won't be easy, I know it will be achievable because I now know who I am as a writer and who I am as a non-writer and am able to use that knowledge to behave more successfully as a writer.

It is this simple process of analyzing, looking for the patterns, and then aggregating that will allow you to build your own habits of asking the questions in this book and thereby embracing the behaviors that build the capabilities at the heart of transformation. Here's a simpler, question-driven version of what I have just outlined. Ask yourself:

1 When I have been successful at something like this, what happened?
2 How can I repeat those patterns?
3 What happens when I do that, what do I learn about me?

The first question is where you analyze, the second is where you aggregate, the third is where you try it and then step back to debrief yourself and cement what you have just learned. From there you just need to follow that rhythm of doing what has worked and seeing if it does again. Do, and then reflect. Do, and then reflect. This will be the heartbeat of your heart of transformation.

Finding your pacemakers for your heart of transformation

Hopefully you don't think I am "overegging the pudding," as my English friends say, by continuing on with the heart metaphors. I just happen to think that what we are talking about here goes beyond just maxims or processes and into ways of being and working that are core to who we are as individuals and human beings. Being a transformative leader, or person, is something that lives inside of you and aligns with what you feel matters as a human being. It is about caring, about hope, about the joy that there can be in growth, learning, and changing. And so, I stick with the heart because that is where my ability to change comes from.

But sometimes the heart needs help. There are two big categories of your heart of transformation helpers—individuals and groups— and you can find and engage with them in different ways. In this next section we will talk about how you get that help but, before we do, I want to talk about help in general, asking for it and receiving it.

Help. It is a fascinating topic. We all need it and yet we struggle to ask for it. In fact, the more successful we are the more likely we are to be reticent to ask for help. I am not talking about asking people to do things we cannot do, or complete tasks we assign to them. I am talking about asking people to help us do what we do, or what we now need to do, better. Invariably, after I get to know my clients, what they say they have come to value most about our relationship is not the subject-matter expertise I bring them or the advice I offer them, but the help I provide them in preserving their thinking time. In the classic 2002 *Harvard Business Review* article "Beware the Busy Manager," the researchers say what is below about the top 10 percent of managers, whom they call the purposeful manager. The researchers are looking at the biggest differences between the purposeful manager and the other types. They talk about the constraints that non-purposeful managers feel subject to such as those around them and their role descriptions. They let these outside forces impact their thinking on what they feasibly can and cannot do. The researchers go on to say that these non-purposeful managers take these perceived constraints into account when:

> they're deciding what's feasible and what isn't. In other words, they work from the outside in. Purposeful managers do the opposite. They decide first what they must achieve and then work to manage the external environment—tapping into resources, building networks, honing skills, broadening their influence—so that, in the end, they meet their goals.[2]

If you reread that you might notice that nowhere does it say that they do it alone. In fact, they specifically reference tapping into resources, building networks, honing skills, and broadening their influence. All of these are things that can or must require others. Earlier in the research article it talks about how these purposeful managers protect their think time. When I was at Gartner, a key success driver of the executive programs service was helping our C-suite clients preserve and use their thinking time in a world of excessive demands and rapidly increasing and changing expectations. As the compensation of our leaders has grown greater and as their scope of authority and resources has grown wider and deeper, we seem to have concomitantly said to them something along the lines of, "And you better do it on your own if we're paying you this much!" We have created leaders who are so lauded and richly rewarded for being all things to all people that we have made it hard for them to ask for help.

The value of thinking time to a heart of transformation

I will never forget an early coaching moment I had with one of the top technology executives of one of the world's most famous and revered financial services firms. I was relatively new to coaching very senior leaders but had been asked in to do this by someone who worked for me and thought I would be a great fit for this leader. We had taken a stroll around the New York City waterfront one day at lunch time. I had spent the time asking her some questions, listening, playing back what I heard, and then letting her continue to speak. Inside, I started to become a nervous wreck. It seemed to me that all she was doing was saying out loud to me things that she already knew and had said in her own head to herself before. As this continued, I began to believe that there was no way this was valuable to her. Quite the opposite; in fact, as we walked and talked I began to be convinced that I was probably just aggravating her but that she was being nice and not saying so. By the end of the hour, I was thoroughly convinced that this was the last time she would ever agree to meet with me. But, as I had been taught as a coach, when we reached the end of the conversation, I swallowed my worries about my value and asked her, "So, what was most useful about our conversation today?"

I waited for the hammer to fall. "Well," she started, "you picked out from what I said a couple of good ideas about what I could do next. And you also had me say out loud things that I've been thinking for some time." I responded, "Yes, sorry I could not have helped you figure out more of what to do or come up with something more original and useful." She paused and looked at me curiously. "I think you misunderstand me if you think that I am not happy with that. Please understand that I can go days, I can go weeks, without anyone giving me two good, actionable ideas to effectively deal with the things I've been struggling with. I am delighted with this. Furthermore, you got me to say out loud things that have been in my head for some time. But, somehow, saying them out loud to you made them so much more real and helped me see so much more clearly what I need to do next. This has, frankly, been one of the most useful and productive hours I've spent in I don't know how many weeks. Can we meet again?"

You could have picked up my jaw from the flagstone paving. I have often thought of that moment so many years ago when I am working with my clients today. It taught me that smart people need help. Not by people smarter than them but by people willing to help them think. People who will ask them the questions they might even have started to ask internally. By playing back what you hear them say and seeing how it sounds to them. By letting them have their thinking time. My greatest joy with a client is that moment when they start a sentence, usually after a pause, with something to the effect of "Ah, I just realized…" It really doesn't matter what it was they realized, what matters is that they made a new realization, they broke through on finding or solving a problem. What matters to me is I created the interpersonal process that allowed for that. You may remember this from very early on in this book when we talked about Ed Schein and process consulting. That's what help is all about.

Getting help with your thinking time for
a heart of transformation

Let's look now at how this story applies to you as a leader or to the leaders you work with. We all need those people who will be there to help us preserve our thinking time and to be with us as we strive to think, learn, grow, do more, and be more. This can be informal or very formal, or both is maybe even better. But start with whatever you have. If you are a senior leader who can afford to find and engage an executive coach who approaches their client relationships from this perspective, then engage them. If you have resources in your HR or OD departments who do this well, then work with them. If you have peers that you trust, then you can create a mutual coaching relationship with them. One of the best coaching relationships I ever had was with my friend and colleague David Meredith. David worked for me, but I was smart enough to realize that in eight out of ten organizations I'd probably be working for him and realized what an asset I had in him. While I was his manager, we did have the same hierarchical manager to managed relationship that you would expect in many appropriate ways. But we also had a unique side to what we did that was not so traditional for our respective roles, where we chose Humanizing Before Organizing.

David had honed his, already admirable, coaching skills through programs I had brought to Gartner. And, I am pleased to say, he probably equaled or even surpassed his teachers in short order when it came to his coaching skills. He is an outstanding coach. So, we made an agreement. Once a month we left the office environment and went somewhere neutral. We didn't meet with him sitting in the guest chair across my imposing wooden desk. Instead, we would grab a sandwich in the cafeteria or go for a walk. Then, we would inhabit entirely new roles for the next hour. In that hour he was my coach, not one of my employees. He would ask questions and I would allow myself to be helped. We built our own cone of confidentiality around the subject matter so I could be totally honest and open with him and, when the hour was over, he acted (publicly and privately) as if what we had talked about had never been spoken of, even when it impacted him or his peers as my employees. It was some of the best, most consistent coaching I have ever received. David and I remain close friends today and I can always count on him when I need help thinking something through.

As you can see, there are a lot of ways to find those people who will act as your process consultants, helping you keep the space to think and figure out what you need to do on your journey to growing your heart of transformation. It is a personal journey, but it is not one you need do alone. It is your individual responsibility, but others can help you as you decide how to best shoulder it. And don't forget, there are also some important people out there who are not your coach, who are not your consultant. They are just the people who care about you and love you and remind you that you have succeeded and grown before and will do it again. They are valuable too. It takes love and caring to grow a heart of transformation.

Finding your thinking group for a heart of transformation

There is another way to be helped as you embark upon the heart of transformation journey and this is with a group. Some of you may be lucky enough to be reading this as part of a program in your organization, as mentioned earlier. If so, then you probably already have a cohort that you are a part of who are being given tools and help to support each other. But you don't need to be doing that to find your own personal advisory board for work and life. Just think about who you might assemble together, if you could, to talk to and hear what they have to say. People who would be willing to tell you how they perceive and experience you and be honest about it; good, bad, and indifferent. I have regularly made the trip to Toronto over the years to sit with two of the best and brightest friends I have, to tell them what is happening and just hear them reflect back to me what they hear and see. It has been invaluable. I have also pulled together small groups in my workplace to do this for me, and we almost always end up doing it for each other. Our little "work therapy" sessions build a sense of trust and belonging that we all find sustaining as we struggle through the challenges of leading and changing and finding our best selves. There are probably some great ways to do this online, I have just not done that yet (although I have held these helping support groups over video conference, for sure.) In whatever manner you choose to proceed, just proceed. Find those people that you think can play a role in helping you grow and nurture your heart of transformation to a strong and vibrant one. The best part is, you will likely end up helping them just as much as they help you. It just seems to be that way when we put our hearts out there for each other.

Tools for transformation—building heart health

We are coming close to the end. I have done my best to give you all the swimming strokes I have when it comes to growing a strongly beating heart of transformation in your chest and to building one inside your organization (or many organizations) as a result. If you visit me on my website at michaelleckie.com you will find a continually growing set of downloadable tools and other resources for just about every idea in this book, and then some. And if you don't find what you need, please let me know. If I can build it for you, and therefore for others, I will.

As I have said many times before, change and transformation is personal. It starts with you, no one else. I guess maybe I could have called this book *Your Heart of Transformation*. I chose not to because this is, despite some appearances, not a self-help book. It is a helping-others-through-helping-yourself-first book. If you are a leader it is written to you but not for you, it is for those that you are privileged to lead. If you are a practitioner it is not for you, it is for those whom you are called to help lead and those they lead. Don't mistake me, I am thrilled that it may end up being something truly and deeply useful to you as an individual human being. And I fervently wish that it ends up improving the lives of those you work with at all levels.

I'd love to hear from you how useful it was, and I'd also love to hear what could have been better. While the book you've read is finished, our collective journeys are far from over and what has been written here is not the end of the story. Stories will be added. More people will come up with more and better ways to build hearts of transformation in themselves and their companies. A community will, hopefully, rise from this book and become a source of support and inspiration that continually evolves and strengthens. I'd be very happy for you to join me in building strong hearts of transformation in all the places they would make the world better (which is just about everywhere)!

Believe in the joy of your own inadequacy. Humility and curiosity are the beating chambers of a heart of transformation. Your heart drives your actions and motion. Your action and motion keep your heart healthy and growing. Having a strong heart of transformation is no different from the physical heart in that sense. Stay strong, stay heart strong, and change your world for good!

Your story is still being written

You may have noticed that all of the capabilities chapters in this book started with a story and more have followed. Sometimes I may have introduced you to the people who are in, or who brought to me, the stories I told. Sometimes they may have already been well known to you. There are, of course, other great examples out there that illustrate the six capabilities, but I chose the ones I had a personal connection to for a reason. Each and every one of these people I have learned something from. Some I have learned a great deal from, some just enough. Some I have known for years; some are new to me. What they all have in common is that they are part of the collection of people in my life that I treasure.

I have had some wonderful opportunities and experiences in my life. I have worked hard. I have studied and received a wonderful education from some of the best teachers in the world. I was gifted with enough native intelligence to be able to do very well in our world. And, probably more than I even realize, I have benefited from the privilege of being a straight, white, cisgender male growing up in the United States during a time of relative prosperity and peace in a middle-class household with two parents who loved me.

Many of my friends are similar, this is what happens with the impact of proximity on relationships in life. But there are also many who came from very different places to get where they are in their life. I value them all. As I have grown and gained experience and a reputation for what I do or have done, I have done my best not only to continue to build those relationships but to be open to new ones. Now, of course, we only have so many hours in the day. But if someone reaches out to me, I will always consider if this is an opportunity where I can make a connection with them and help them and see if more of a relationship is in the cards. I find it interesting that many of these contacts that turn into friendships happen through LinkedIn. I find that interesting because LinkedIn is a daily source of faux-personal business spam that is clearly meant to sound personal to me and is anything but. It is too often, through no fault of its own, a source of a frequent and disrespectful waste of the only resource I can never replenish, my time. But I still look at my inbox because it led me to people like Ilkka Mäkitalo and Jouko Virtanen, Hilton Barbour, Olivia D'Silva, and others too numerous to mention here.

The fact of the matter is that I am only as good as the people I learn from. As you look at applying what you have learned in this book—asking the questions, stepping back to learn from them, building new habits—consider that it is never enough and that you will only go so far on your own. Learning and growth, like change, need the richness of the input, support, guidance, example, and presence of others to really take hold and last. It is those people around you who will prompt you forward when you tire. They will hold you accountable when you fall short. They will remind you what good looks like (and sometimes not-so-good, which is probably just as useful if not more). They will be there to just love you no matter what you do, say, or accomplish.

In addition to using the stories of, or from, real people I know to illustrate the value of others in your life, there is another reason for it. Change is personal. While some of the changes talked about in this book are enormous—the cultural shift at Microsoft, for example—they happened because of individuals. You can only make change, whether to individuals, teams, groups, organizations, or continents, one person at a time. One individual person at a time. You cannot categorize and lump them together and then throw out one big bone that all will run towards. You have to engage them in their change by understanding where they are now, having respect for their right to be who they are now, and working with them to help them ask themselves good questions that might help them learn (unless it is you who has to do the learning... maybe a little of both?).

To repeat my frequent admonition: start with you. That is enough. Ask yourself these questions as you ask them of others. Learn, and then share what you've learned. Change some habits. You are the most powerful vehicle for change you have, don't take yourself for granted. Don't let your heart weaken and compromise the impact you are meant to have on your world. Build a strong heart of transformation and change your world. For good.

Endnotes

1 Rose, T (2016) *The End of Average: How we succeed in a world that values sameness*, Harper Onc, San Francisco CA

2 Bruch, H and Ghoshal, S (2002) Beware the Busy Manager [online] https://store.hbr.org/product/beware-the-busy-manager/r0202d?sku=R0202D-PDF-ENG (archived at https://perma.cc/6JGU-GJRM)

INDEX

From 4 December 2025 the EU Responsible Person (GPSR) is:
eucomply oÜ, Pärnu mnt. 139b – 14, 11317 Tallinn, Estonia
www.eucompliancepartner.com

www.ingramcontent.com/pod-product-compliance
Lightning Source LLC
Chambersburg PA
CBHW041208220326
41597CB00030BA/5115